* * * * * * * * * * * * * *

* *" THE RING OF FRIENDS:* *
* *FOREVER"* *

* *

* *POEM COLLECTION* *

* *BY FLORENCE ROSIE GIVENS* *

* * * * * * * * * * * * * * *

Author Florence Rosie Givens

* * * * * * * * * * * * * * * * *

"A Morning Without Coffee" © 2000
" Revisiting Friends: The Journey Home" © 2001
" The Ring Of Friends: Forever" © 2002

A Special Feature of
****Author's Brief Personal History ****
My Life, Dreams and Aspirations
(At the Beginning of This Book)

**** America's Victory after The Attack Poems ****
September 11,2001 Bringing A Closure For America
Dedicated to The Lost, Victims, Survivors and
Person of the Year 2001 Mayor Rudolph W. Giuliani, NY
Also to Governor George Pataki, NY
(At The Conclusion of This Book)

" THE RING OF FRIENDS: FOREVER "

POEM COLLECTION BY FLORENCE ROSIE GIVENS

Author/ Editor
Florence Rosie Givens

"The Ring Of Friends: Forever "
Poem Collection
By Florence Rosie Givens

Library of Congress Control Number: 2002100584
ISBN 0-9705819-2-0

Printed in the United States of America
Fredericksburg, VA. USA
First Edition
Author Editor Publisher Florence Rosie Givens

Published by:
FloBound Poems
Florence Rosie Givens
P.O. Box 3101
Fredericksburg, VA. 22402
www.floboundpoems.com (For Orders)
MorningPoemsFloG@ aol.com

(Orders) Bookstores:
www.amazon.com
Gospel and Gifts Towne Books
2852 Ste. # 103 Jefferson Davis Hwy.
Stafford, VA. USA 22554
1-800-720-1720
www.gospelandgifts.com

Front Cover Design by Jared M. Stark **www.digraphics.com**
Back Cover Photo by Florence Rosie Givens

Other Published Books By Florence Rosie Givens
" A Morning Without Coffee" Poem Collection © 2000
" Revisiting Friends: The Journey Home" © 2001

Dedication

This book is dedicated to:

My Proud Sponsors 2002
My Children, My Friends:
Anderson Jackson, Jr.
Freda A. Jackson-Nelson
Gregory T. Wright, Sr.
Mario D. Jackson

Also, Husband and Friend,
Josephus Givens, Jr.

Thank You Family

" Friends Forever"
Feeling right at home
Realizing that you're loved
Identified amongst strangers
Enduring hardship together
Never letting go of hope
Delightful conversations in life
Seldom feeling left out

Fresh ideas come easy
Oneness for all of life
Revisit loved ones, friends
Entering into a happy state
Victory in the life you live
Everyone needs to converse
Remember family and friends
Friends Forever

The Ring Of Friends: Forever

Life have been grand, I have survived thus far, and my whole life is better for it...now that I understand...patience, endurance... steadfastness, tolerance, and suffering...but not alone...for Jesus, Family, Friends, and others stood right there with me and for me ...and I know they all meant well.

As you read further into this book you will comprehend the power of a mother caring for her four children as a single parent yet was able by God's help...to help others on this life journey...and survived with a will to print it in a book of poetry.

This book is about going on with one's life and surviving the odds......that show up in our lives...not always by choice but that... it is beyond our control, yet we must brush off our knees and go on...with our life.

It serves as a variety of poetry, and words of wisdom...found in pages of ... "Speaking To Your Heart In A Pause." The pauses will be for an enlightenment of cares, and gives one a pause from the rhymes, and the rhythm of ...poetry itself. *Florence Rosie Givens*

Introduction

"What does it matter?" as I say to myself, as I sit here in the middle of washing dishes. This instance was so important that I had to stop, to jot down the ideas for this collection of poetic work. When the flow of words, are as a river, set the pail, get the pen, and the pad for on that note, you're in for the story of your life. And, this is what I intend to tell to others, how I survived.....and pressed my way to where I am.

Not by failure but by determination of will, by integrity of the mind by rubies and jewels found in people, by God's grace and mercy... and most of all by Jesus' love for us all.

The scene here is set, stage curtains opened, and will not close until I have told my story... and above all, have survived.

Let's drop in, a porcelain tub, on legs in the corner of the bathroom with issues of life now pressing upon the door. With the family background of dignity, respect, character and integrity...there's never room, for a pity-party. For, people will read and need your story, on every day. "Why?"There should be no why?

You can't live and go on with your life, as I have by asking yourself that question, let..... alone, asking God that question. Don't ask... God why?...His Deity speaks for Itself, He's All Knowing, and He's knows all the answers ...stay with God...and you'll get somewhere.

We can only get there, in a positive sense of which, if you're not positive, you will not do positive things in life, as go on, with your life.

Things are not really that bad, stay in the world that God put you in, and don't go off into your own world, unless you can handle it. You can handle it, by fighting negatives, and downsizing of friends (when you really need them the most, and are at your worst).

In life, you'd best have enough confidence in yourself, or, you'd best get to people very quickly to see if you can get encouragement. Yes, this sounds like another......"There she goes again" just someone who... thinks they know life, by far, I not only know just a little something...but I've lived a little something.

Let's keep moving here, for the world and society will catch up to us, and we have to be at least a few steps ahead....in order to make it through...in this tough cruel world.

You sit with friends, and talk, but now it's your turn. You, God, a pen, and pad....dear hearts, minds, and many listening ears ready to pass along the message. Better yet, buy a book for your friends, and let them decipher for themselves, and grasp more hope, in life as needed for this journey of freedom.

Don't wait for people to jump out and help you ...help yourself, after all it's your life.... tell your story, above all, live it all in victory.

You have your own slot in life, and what a person says or does......won't take your slot away, unless you allow it. Be strong, subdue hardness as a good soldier, with God by your side. On the side of being in the limelight, "if you want to come along, you're welcomed."

Introduction

As goes the saying, feel welcomed to come venture along, and the old adage says "If not don't hinder me." There's a lot of people in life to speak of here, so I'll keep it at a mere minimum, that way no one will feel that they have been talked about in this book. This... book is about whosoever wants to go on with their life. Whosoever wants to... "Come Up From Where You Are," poem quoted in the book, *"A Morning Without Coffee."* *© 2000*

People will talk for hours, about writing a book, after, their children grow up, or after they find out how, or when they'll have the finances...there's no magical moment for... book publishing, self-publish or otherwise.

As in furthering education it simply must be done, or hope that your enthusiasm holds out over the doubts. We pay more.... for an automobile, than we do for self-publishing books......have confidence in God, yourself, and in your work, and be diligent.

I'm excited about life,God, family, friends, writing, and all of the positive things in life. I love to uplift people, and find that if I can get writers, poets, enthused as I've been ..... enthused then they can get published.

Writing makes...a place of solitude for its writer. Yet now, a writer has surfaced with poetry for your reading pleasure let's go on along this journey in ease of character.

The poems here and in the other books are written about every day life, in various styles, and have been reviewed...as superb poetry.

The Ring Of Friends: Forever

There comes a time in life that we draw a conclusion and come to a crossroad...and must, walk the road of life alone, as I was told years ago, by my natural father, that on the road of life we have... family and friends but, the decisions at the crossroad ...must be ours.

Being that it's all a part of growing up ... I came out ahead in growing up fast after the walk in life with trials and tests at a... younger age...does it matter about age, or the vast part in which we live? I think not, for it took a very strong constitution, and the will to move on...with God's love, grace and mercy toward my family and me.

This is just the beginning of a story... that may enhance, and touch your life in a.... positive, and realistic way. Another chapter has been filled in my life...and I feel good... about life...for I have Jesus, family, friends, that have supported me in more ways than I can name.

I go on, feeling "Inspired"...."Enthused"... with dreams fulfilled in writing nine books of poetry, and publishing three...I have a story to tell, and perhaps this will encourage someone to go on and tell their story as well.

Florence Rosie Givens

Preface

Back by Popular Demand: also Author of
"A Morning Without Coffee" © 2000
" Revisiting Friends: The Journey Home" © 2001
See with wisdom advise with love. By doing so you will have gain. Friends are as family and family as friends...reach them by... a measure of faith and love.

The Ring Of Friends: Forever
Poem Collection © 2002

Smiles are coming your way today,......catch the enthusiasm. When you reach out to friends in life you show them by example that you are friendly ...a friend found makes a happy heart ...a friend kept makes life easier to get through. Use this book "The Ring Of Friends: Forever" as a companion...read with an open mind and imagine the position in life you hold dear with friends. Write with enthusiasm... talk with a positive mind...walk with steadfastness...and run with the grace of God.

As you read allow your mind to be free...find some comfort in poetry. Poetry cleanses out doubt, bringing... a peaceful heart and mind. Comfort in... "The Ring Of Friends: Forever" is sought with hope and...will be defined by many people worldwide... as friends share this book with family and friends. Expectations in life drives one to search for happiness ...read with values of fine wisdom.....and find many revelations of love.

Florence Rosie Givens
Author / Publisher

Acknowledgements

Firsthand I acknowledge the Lord's great blessings upon my life allowing me to... accomplish this endeavor. I wish to thank the following persons for their assistance, conversation, friendship and encouragement:

* *

With love and special thanks to you,
****Josephus Givens, Jr., my husband, friend by my side, wishing me the best in life.***
Love and Special Thanks My Sponsors:
****Anderson Jackson, Jr.***
****Freda A. Jackson-Nelson***
****Gregory T. Wright, Sr.***
****Mario D. Jackson***

* *

Sheridan Books, Inc.
Marcel Southern
Debbie Tremper
Cathy McAtee Luick
The Free Lance Star
Cathy Dyson
Gospel and Gifts
Robert Jenkins, Jr.
Beatrice Green
Digraphics
Jared M. Stark
Burr Hill Gifts & Ceramics
Catherine Edwards
Bonnie Lea Loving
Raymond L. Camp
Thelma L. Camp
My Child Left Behind Org.
Shirley Howell
Oprah Winfrey
Paul & Jan TBN
Alexandria Gazette
Gale Curcio
Louise Krafft
Claude Williams
Kathy Adams
Mary W. Porter
Donald Minor
Iredell Jenkins
Fleur M. Beauchamp
Eva M. Daniels
Dorothy B. Walters
Mary V. Coleman
Barbara C. Camp
Woolfolk Publications
Thomas Woolfolk
Amazon.com & Others

" Poems "

Soothing words as the flowing of a water brook upon the meadows. Erasing doubts, easing heartaches. Softly, yet strongly read.

When you can't be there, with friends, send them a personal copy of poetry and wisdom: "The Ring Of Friends: Forever" © 2002 Poem Collection By Florence Rosie Givens

Surround a friend with love, peace and harmony

"The Ring Of Friends: Forever "

Family, friends, and others want to express their concerns, interest as friendly supporter, of this book…I'm thankful. *Florence Rosie Givens*

On the following page, find true expressions of love…and pure friendship…some from far, some from near…yet they have expressed words that touch my heart…in lovely ways. *F.R.G.*

Look across the page and enjoy the journey… for the best… is yet to come…even after you read this book, a few more friends…may show up. May they be real and true...is my wish. *F.R.G.*

*The Penmanship Page......................... **

Find the road to fine poetry as others have, and be... uplifted by these books.

"A Morning Without Coffee"
"Revisiting Friends: The Journey Home"
".........Positively inspiring."
- Freda A. Nelson, Virginia, USA

"In life God allows us to go through some situations so that we will depend upon Him. Serving Jesus Christ as Lord and Saviour allows us to find peace in the midst of life's... many storms.

The poems written by Florence Jackson-Givens allows one to see a woman who no matter the situation.....depended upon God and found peace in the storm.

Florence's writing enables one to....see that God does not have favorites when it comes to equipping us with His gifts.

Having read *"A Morning Without Coffee"*... and *"Revisiting Friends: The Journey Home,"* I was able to see a woman grow spiritually in Christ. In addition, I was able to see a sweet peace that surpasses all earthly understanding."
- Dameron L. Jones, Germantown, MD 20874

** The Penmanship Page.............(Cont'd)*

Find the road to fine poetry as others have, and be... uplifted by these books.

"I met Flo via the Internet. Our connection was poetry. Flo has become my Bestest and Friendliest Friend.
She has lived life. She has survived life. She has embraced life.
Flo embraces her friends in the same manner - with encompassing love and wisdom- both of which she shares happily.

This newest book of specially created and chosen poetry extends her embrace......to a larger circle of friends, old and new.

Read these wonderful poems and relax, feel her friendly hug- her encircling warmth. Relationships are the most important aspects of life. Feel this, develop this......as you read these poems and apply them to your life.
Life is a circle. Friendship spirals on- many circles within a circle.
A hug is a circle. Pass it on. And pass on the news of this great book*"The Ring Of Friends: Forever"* by Florence Rosie Givens."

"Flo, you are in my estimation, the Greatest and every effort you make towards your goals proves it. Therefore, your every success counts as a major stride."
- Fleur M. Beauchamp, Teacher
Kemptville, Ontario, Canada

*The Penmanship Page..............(Cont'd)**

Find the road to fine poetry as others have, and be... uplifted by these books.

"My dear friend Flo has written another book of poetry, ... *"The Ring Of Friends: Forever,"* wherein the reader feels uplifted and wiser after reading each poem.

This is rare.... and often hard searched for these days. It is with joy that I write this little forward. It is a singular honour to be associated with poetry of this genre.

This book is a warm spirit –raiser, and ... soul -hugger collection of warmth and wisdom. Pop it into your pocket or purse to... browse through whenever you have a spare minute and the desire to pamper yourself."
- Fleur M. Beauchamp, Teacher
Kemptville, Ontario, Canada

"Florence, it is always a bright spot in my day when I get an e-mail from you. You are always so up beat and cheerful it is like a ray of sunshine peeking through the window shade! You are truly a jewel standing out on ...a beach of sand."
- Candice M. Otto, Ocala, Florida, USA

**** The Penmanship Page.............(Cont'd)***

Find the road to fine poetry as others have, and be... uplifted by these books.

I enjoy having, *"A Morning Without Coffee"* and *"Revisiting Friends: The Journey Home"* on my coffee table to share with...my friends. It is strange, that we have never met outside this computer box, and yet it is as if our souls have known each other for an eternity. You are a ray of sunshine breaking through a dark cloud, I absorb the warmth of your sunshine. Thank you......You lighten my heart.
- Candice M. Otto, Ocala, Florida, USA

" A Poem for Florence Rosie Givens "

Florence, has a special gift from above, a talent with words like no other,
She has been through such hard times and all the while remains a wonderful person... and a mother.
No one will ever find Florence....without a kind word or a smile,
No matter what or who the "asking" would be, she would kindly and patiently walk that extra mile.
She writes poems from "Her heart,"....that touch "The heart."
God has put many angels on earth to protect and guide us, and...Florence Rosie Givens is truly one, for all ...and everyone of us.

- Bonnie Lea Loving, Virginia, USA

"The Ring Of Friends: Forever"

" Cleansing Of A Poem "

**We have need of encouragement,
in God's people, and His Word,
Sometimes we need an example of
lovely ways after all we've heard.**

**You could read text books and of
course you could learn,
You could read novels and you may
have a concern.**

**Sometimes a lyric or two won't hurt
your morale,
Sometimes a friend, family or a kind
word from a pal.**

**But if you want a natural cleansing
that is of a norm,
You need to read....soothing words
with the "Cleansing Of A Poem."**

**It may help get you pass heartaches
and pain, set upon your endeavors,
Now you know how others feel when
you say "Read poems? Oh, I never!"**

***Readers, Writers, Poets, Artists,
Musicians, and All.....Enjoy the
essence of Poetry at last, as....
happy flowing verses...flow on.***

CONTENTS

CONTENTS CONT'D

CONTENTS CONT'D

CONTENTS CONT'D

CONTENTS CONT'D

CONTENTS CONT'D

CONTENTS CONT'D

CONTENTS CONT'D

***Poems Bringing A Closure For America * Cont'd-**

*** Poems Bringing A Closure For America Ends***

*** Other Every Day Poetry and Words Of Wisdom ***

*** Speaking To Your Heart In A Pause ***

CONTENTS CONT'D

Speaking To Your Heart In A Pause ....

We're all busy with family, jobs or what have you, yet time always permits a place for friends. There's very lonely people out there needing love, and a caring kind voice, to not merely, to talk, but to spread cheer.

We're sometimes bogged down to cares, that we often are relieved from, only by a corner of solitude. If and when we find this corner, converse and pray for strength, for it is found in quietness and peace.

When you return to the busy world, you would have accomplished, a peace of mind, after a victorious corner talk with God.

Everyone wants the comfort zone and the peaceful ways of others to flow out to them. It's not always in the comfort of life, that we find strength, so we do press on higher.

At times it's great to ask....."Lord, what are you saying unto us?" At times, it's not always in others, for the answer is, in us.

We do have a history of friends, let's say ...good friends, it seems better on the mind that way. Time does have a way, of refreshing the wonders it so dearly permit, along with many lovely experiences that do come.

What friendship does bring to our lives is so very wholesome, and the universe has been freely placed there for vibes of love.

End the day with a pleasant undertaking of a reality search, and feeling good about the accomplishments of the day's moments. What fares better in life than having a very pleasant day.....in a direction of friendship.

Speaking To Your Heart In A Pause ....

When we open up to the universe, and... allow our hearts to be so kind, an excellent thing happens. People begin to take notice and will go out of their way... just to greet you, even...with only a smile.

We can falter in life if we don't stay on... the positive side of things......we must say, we're not going to accept it and thereby the attitudes change and miracles happen. It... feels so good to be in a state of peace, love and being aware, of our surroundings and other people's feelings.

Everyone may not show that they...really love us or even care...yet go on...it's always yet go on, and that's what we will do. Find happiness, understanding, and...a peaceful happy face, through it all.

At times people say "Get a life!".....and in a positive sense it means...yet go on...you've got to make it all right. We know if we keep reminding ourselves that we're blessed, and strong, encouraged......then we will be what our emotions press upon us.

When love steps in, things seem to....work better, people smile, and things will move at whatever pace...but they move. On that note we realize that we must move the wall, fence or whatever blocks the friendship of friends or family. Let's rethink the principles of life yet, keep the old ways....the good paths. We do live in the same world, and can all try to make this a much better world, that we live in by...embracing life and friendship.

"The Ring Of Friends: Forever" A book so inspiring...that even if you didn't have a friend...you would end up being a friend to... yourself, after reading it. We need to be.... inspired.

This time you would want your own copy...there's no telling where your personal copy will end up. Some of us love reading, writing, and you've come to the right place for richness of peaceful wording.....and yet you can get the right point, of the story.

When you read about your enemies and feel good about them and yourselves, then you're on the road to a great awareness of yourself, that we must love them anyhow...and yet go on with our lives.

After reading, a portion of this book and you feel good about enemies... after all, they pay not you, then how good are you going to feel, about.... your friends? It's your decision, as you read on in hope....feel inspired.

We know that our families, and our friends, should make us... feel good about life, and living, and we should do the same for them....as we're into "The Ring Of Friends: Forever."

-Florence Rosie Givens

" A Pen Of Hope "

**Writing solidly through trials at best,
Coping words to help pass the test.
Led by God and His inspiring love,
All written of ink, coming from above.
Reading words inspiring the universe,
Sounding better now, as we rehearse.
Writing with a quality of love,
Reading with wisdom from God above.**

The blessing of the Lord, it maketh rich, and
he addeth no sorrow with it. Proverb 10:22 KJV

They helped everyone his neighbour; and
every one said to his brother, Be of good
courage. Isaiah 41:6 KJV

The Lord is my strength and song, and is
become my salvation. Psalm 118:14 KJV

" Grocery Lists "

**Getting to know your friends...
Rising to the occasion of love...
Only thing that helps us, love...
Centering your hopes and dreams
Eating what's makes you healthy
Reaching for the blue sky.......
You, me and a world of friends**

**Loving everyone across the board
Increasing your territory.........
Staying in the realm of peace.....
Taking time for yourself.........
Staying delivered in happiness...**

" The Ring Of Friends: Forever "
Poem 1

Since when we've always had friends we really adore,
We've also had friends we like to be in the presence of more.
All along the while through childhood with grace,
Every chance we got we used it to converse and keep up the pace.

College or whatever may have been... the case we reached our goal,
And now to have this opportunity to... greatly and dearly behold.
Behold the goodness that our presence unfolds for free, behold the peace and love, you being you, and me being me.

At last a permanent time that will ever last, becoming "The Ring Of Friends: Forever" and remarkably fast.
Wherever you go, they will follow you along in their minds and heart,
Even when being separated, by states or countries bringing them apart.

One day we'll meet, and refresh the... ideas of a dear friend, never let it pass you by, let it be "The Ring Of Friends: Forever," and never end.

" The Ring Of Friends: Forever "
Poem 2

From childhood we softly and heartily reached out to love,
We loved all the quietness, and the kindness as of a dove.

Our minds went from the days of youth to an older frame,
Of all of our friends we can still find and remember a name.

We've often forgotten faces as our dear knowledge fades,
Yet we keep the hope that our friends have made.

We can only touch "The Ring Of Friends: Forever" because of our heart,
And all the distance will never keep us friends apart.

We'll call, or somehow find each other as our paths cross once more,
And we will be enriched in power of what the Lord has in store.

"The Ring Of Friends: Forever" will be just what it states,
For it will take more for us as the glorious future awaits.

Editor's Note

The poems written in *"The Ring Of Friends: Forever"* is for mental and spiritual digestion. There's no need as I see it to write to you in the language of negatives, we know those all too well in life.

We sometimes want smooth, soothing, happy, inspiring poems without suspense characters that lurk and jump out at us in negative ways. Negative alters the feelings of peacefulness and it disturbs the mind, heart and soul. It drains one's resources of encouragement......let go of all negatives.

The poems here are loyal to a peaceful resolve and are smoothly portrayed without the beginning or ending bearing on the thoughts...except in soft tones of happiness.

All the world could use poetry such as this.... not only that, all the world needs it...spread the wonderful word.

I'd rather say the glass is half full than half empty. To remind someone I'd rather say "Try to remember" rather than, "Don't forget." I'd rather say "It's nice to see you".... rather than "My, you've gained weight"or "You look sick." After all, we all need uplifting. If a person did look sick it would most nearly cause more hardship to them to speak negatively to them.

It would benefit the both of you to spare the feelings of each other. Thereby the friendship is more rewarding and time will have its place for coincidence and causes for concern....find some kind words to say.

In order to cheer people up, you must have a spirit to lift them up.You must first have this spirit yourself then let it spread to others....If you want a "pick me up" you will find it here, for the purpose of writing here is to uplift and build with insight and wisdom.

The poems here will be a friend when you're lonely and a companion when your spirits are low.....as you allow yourself to believe in yourself and in your decisions.

I would think that the reason that you are now reading this book is to get more insight, uplift, inspiration, or an answer to ordinary everyday situations that may have pressed upon your mind.

You have come to the right place for you.... will with hope find comfort,"mindful of feelings" poetry, and will hopefully feel better after this session of reading than before you started.

Please refer this book "*The Ring Of Friends: Forever*" to your....family, friends, co workers, your stockbroker. Also, anyone that will benefit from the uplift of the poetry written here and in: "*A Morning Without Coffee,*""*Revisiting Friends: The Journey Home.*"

***"The Ring Of Friends: Forever"* is in essence... the cream of the crop of three published books by Florence Rosie Givens. It was born out of "*A Morning Without Coffee," and "Revisiting Friends: The Journey Home.*"**

The author's style is freely expressed, and has reached many, and yet many, is to be reached by the writer's capture of minds as they are absorbed in pleasant moments of reading.

The poems here are everyday life like poetry that is self explanatory and to the point. No wondering about the title for the lines plainly following through brings the point out clearly and .... wholesomely for your reading pleasure..

The poems here has a variety of titles for we must have a variety in our life to balance out a healthy existence. Reading poetry is good for the soul for it brings out a character and a longing to be free of minute cares.

The poems are written from observation of a world in need of attention and freedom. All of the poems are to be read with an individual value in in mind. Keep reading them and get the message from your own heart and mind. Reminisce...with your friends.

The poems here were written after searching for poetry that uplifted smoothly and was soft to feelings that needs a lift rather than a chastening. We, as life goes on know mostly what we need...to utilize our skills to receive it brings about a search... Look here in "*The Ring Of Friends: Forever.*"

Read for yourself and I'd be glad if you'd e-mail your review, and let me know how it may have touched your life and advanced you to another level of harmony.

Feel free to write me at the address in the beginning of the book, and let me know if you'd like to consider copyrighting and/or publish your poetry or novel... take the journey the view is great.The poetry here, I would sincerely hope will enhance your life...it has enhanced mine.

Often I read the poetry here, for its purpose is to uplift and help a person to hopefully come to grip with life's trials and ...move on. I too have moved on with my life, being stagnated causes too much concern.

There's a "yes or no" answer that's searched for and in the poetry in this book it's plainly stated. In life either we will or we won't, it's just a matter of time, whether we will live in this state or another...we can decide.

As you decide on many facets in life, decide on reading good pleasant poetry as in..."*The Ring Of Friends: Forever*" for you will perhaps thank the person that led you to this book.

The poetry here carries a tolerance for short comings in life and in people...love people anyhow, love life because you're free. We must give more sometimes than we receive and that's what this poetry is about.

Line by line it expresses hope and speaks to someone's heart saying hold on things will get better...God willing.

As you pass the gift of *"The Ring Of Friends: Forever"*, it will most certainly be a start in someone's life to see life in a whole new light.

The poems are an expression of things that you may have wanted to say yet, the words didn't flow as freely. As you read you may look upon these poems as a stepping stone to a recovery of will. The will that may have vanished or partially.... vanished because of harsh words of family, friends, co workers...or strangers.

All of the poetry here, are written to be read with ease of mind and heart.They're not meant to be harsh...only caring. I seek such to read so I wrote such...and to bless myself and others along life's journey way.

An older person will benefit from reading..... *"The Ring Of Friends: Forever"* as well as teenagers and middle age persons. Reading these poems will hopefully lift your spirit by many degrees of happiness.

Share a copy with your friend, or if you would not like to depart from this book, purchase one for them also. We like to share good things yet when you need encouragement keep *"The Ring Of Friends: Forever," "Revisiting Friends: The Journey Home,"...*"*A Morning Without Coffee"* on hand for yourself. It's worth the time and price to be uplifted by... Christian type poems, allowing God to administer, His love through the poetry in these books. Reaching also, many disheartened people, and many happy people striving to be happier, pass word of this poem book. Poems that's a blessing, pass on, poems that will only be more seasoned with time as the poetry here...pass it on. Tell people that you've received a blessing, from.... poetry such as this, help a friend to be uplifted, as well as yourself.

If you've read *"A Morning Without Coffee," "Revisiting Friends: The Journey Home,"*...and *"The Ring Of Friends: Forever,"*...and you also have been blessed, you have a reason to share your insight, and referral of this poetry.

The poems here are not written merely just for the author, but to help others see the beauty of good quality poetry. Not only to see the great beauty but experience the beauty of the "ART" of Writing, Poem Collections by Florence Rosie Givens: *A-R-T*

A= "A Morning Without Coffee" © 2000

R= "Revisiting Friends: The Journey Home" © 2001

T= "The Ring Of Friends: Forever" © 2002

The variety of poetry here expresses a need to see the world in a broadminded sense of reasoning. Thereby, wisdom rests upon our minds... and hearts, and we advance in life, and can then keep the fellowship of God...and *"The Ring Of Friends: Forever."* Let's continue to bless ...... friends...making them feel like family and vice versa. Read these books and tell someone how really simple it is to be uplifted by poems in this poetry book.

If we needed a drainpipe repaired, we'd call a plumber, if we needed a room painted we'd certainly call a painter. It's just getting into... the right perspective and then dare to dream.

In essence, if we needed happy, inspiring, and smooth poetry, I would certainly wish that this book, is added to your library. May your days and nights be easier and pleasant. In my own library, alongside my Holy Bible...I add poetry.

God has blessed these poems and I feel uplifted, free, inspired, confident, enriched, encouraged, and delighted in going on with life...come and take this journey in ease as we both use.... these two words...Trust God.

Being in a state of praise, victory, and heartfelt caring for Our Wonderful Creator is an awesome wonder in itself.

To share love, to give love, to receive love, has many characters to be enhanced in our lives.... so many people in need of encouragement everyday...waits for your kindness as friends.

Be it early morning, noon or night, forever be a friend to someone...not leaving out yourself... you're special too.

Reaching the character and personalities of friends is rewarding for it brings out the best in us all...one moment at a time.

In our quietest moments we can grab hold to hope and reason, whilst casting our cares upon God. As close as we are to God we want it in other areas of life for it seems to narrow the... length between friends, and family.

To reach the essence of ultimate glory of love and friendship is like being at the top of a desired mountain. Hope flourishes pass us as we are swept to our feet...on our way to victory land, with a sense of friendship and partnership. The long lasting stand of friendship is never over, it is replenished with everyday life.....as we grow in deeper caring ways.

We know that we can be alone without being lonely... a friendly reminder for some. It's tough to be tenderhearted and tough in life, but it's easier to cope as such...feelings fare better and are less hurt that way.

Putting aside things that cause confusion and ill will brings us closer as friends sometimes we're the one that overlooks someone...and their faults.

23rd Psalm

The Lord is my shepherd; I shall not want.
2 He maketh me to lie down in green pastures:
he leadeth me beside the still waters.
3 He restoreth my soul: he leadeth me in the
paths of righteousness for his name's sake.
4 Yea, though I walk through the valley of the
shadow of death, I will fear no evil: for thou art
with me; thy rod and thy staff they comfort me.
5 Thou prepareth a table before me in the pres-
ence of mine enemies: thou anointest my head
with oil; my cup runneth over.
6 Surely goodness and mercy shall follow me all
the days of my life: and I will dwell in the house
of the Lord for ever.

Psalm 23:1-6 KJV

* * * * * * * * * * * * * * * * * * * ** ** ** ** * * * * * *

The Lord's Prayer

9... Our Father which art in heaven, Hallowed
be thy name.
10 Thy kingdom come. Thy will be done in earth,
as it is in heaven.
11 Give us this day our daily bread.
12 And forgive us our debts, as we forgive our
debtors.
13 And lead us not into temptation, but deliver us
from evil: For thine is the kingdom, and the pow-
er, and the glory, for ever. Amen.

Matthew 6:9-13 KJV

* ** * * ** * ** *

What Jesus Says About Friends: (Excerpts KJV)

13 Greater love hath no man than this, that a man lay down his life for his friends.
14 Ye are my friends, if ye do whatsoever I command you.
15 Henceforth I call you not servants; for the servant knoweth not what his lord doeth: but I have called you friends; for all things that I have heard of my Father I have made known unto you. St John 15:13-15 KJV

* * * * * * * * * * * ** ** ** ** * * * * * * * * * * *

The Friendship Of Ruth and Naomi:(Excerpts KJV)

16 And Ruth said, Intreat me not to leave thee,
or to return from following after thee:for whither thou goeth, I will go; and where thou lodgest, I will lodge:thy people shall be my people, and thy God my God:
17 Where thou diest, will I die, and there will I be
buried: the Lord do so to me, and more also, if ought but death part thee and me. Ruth 1:16,17 KJV

** * * ** * ** *

The Friendship of David and Jonathan: (Excerpts KJV)

And it came to pass, when he had made an end of speaking unto Saul, that the soul of Jonathan was knit with the soul of David, and Jonathan loved him as his own soul.
2 And Saul took him that day, and would not let him go no more home to his father's house.
3 Then Jonathan and David made a covenant, because he loved him as his own soul.
4 And Jonathan stripped himself of the robe that was upon him, and gave it to David, and his garments, even to his sword, and his bow, and to his girdle. I Samuel 18:1-4 KJV *Holy Bible King James Version*

" Hold To Integrity "

It's tough to enter into a happy state in
times of despair,
Yet you can remember the height of the
moon, and meet heaven past there.
You have hope when you heal with time
as it pass by you,
Reach for the Lord, and "Hold To Integrity"
to get you through.
Keep your smiles for you wear them very
well, even though it's day,
For as you "Hold To Integrity" you really
soften your way.
You will get through the night and see the
sunlight upon the day,
As you see the strength in the prayers and
"Hold To Integrity" in every way.
*** ***

" Worthy "

Highly esteemed in a glorious way led of
the morn. Sacrifices fall short of nothing
asked for, obedience is not only heard, but
applied.
Peace and love is expressed to all, God is
in every thought and Heaven is our home.

Only mercy can be expressed when miracles
happen, and Jesus has smiled on us in grace.
The hope is in oneness with God,reassurance
is sought through mercy, grace, and love.
The ways are spiritually expressed, inspired
by a host of scriptures that lives in one's heart.

"Consider Yourself Friendly and Find It"

Search for it upon the hills and the.......
mountaintops, you've reached your goal,
When you have proved your friendliness
and ushered from your heart of old.
You gave good things to your neighbors
and strangers looked at you with a smile,
All the time being enhanced by ....
your loving kindness as of a child.
Show some mercy and compassion that
people may change their ways,
When they look upon your life and notice
that the blessings of God upon you stays.
You have been through storms as well as
anybody else has too,
And it makes for a good example to see the
friendliness expressed in you.
Search for it far and near, seek it everyday
of your life as a friend, people will look to
your life's goodness to help them make it in.
Now it will be a blessing to encourage one
soul to go on their way,
"Consider Yourself Friendly and Find It"
for it will make everything okay.
You will feel more blessed as you reach out
to more friends that you meet,
They will feel the power of love and grace
as you help them stand to their feet.
Look for a friendly personality, and show
others that you can be friendly too,
Not merely as just a person, but a great and
wonderful friend ......through and through.

"Don't Despair"

Have you at any point in life walked alone
and felt omitted?
As long as you are strong stay encouraged,
you won't feel pitied.
You check out your ideas, expressing your
concerns at heart,
Then you say kindly what you feel and not
dwell on it in part.
You're not at a lost,...you've been through
things such as this,
As times go on, you'll find yourself getting
strength as you reminisce.

Let go of concerns, stay in tune to life, and
you'll make it through,
Had it not been thought that you'd benefit,
it wouldn't have come to you.
We learn from life's ups, downs and grow
all the way to the top,
Even from all of the trials, you know that ...
you just don't stop.
Be it a friend or be it a foe, just whisper a
prayer or two,
And "Don't Despair" for good things will
in due time come to you.

A man that hath friends must shew himself friendly: and there is a friend that sticketh closer than a brother. **Proverbs 18:24 KJV**
(Find a Friend...Find Jesus Forever... and He will give you many natural and spiritual friends... that will be friends Forever too.)

Author's Brief Personal History

My Life, Dreams and Aspirations

* *

Theme... "Help Someone Along The Way."

The theme that starts this book is written here in five words. Thus, "*Help Someone Along The Way.*" The curtains here are ... now to be opened, the particles of life are greatly... defined and I am ready to launch a historic view of my life as the love, mercy, and grace of God shine upon me.

I was born to a wonderful set of parents Carrie Mae Camp, and Edward Camp.... My mother was from New York City, USA. My dad was from Virginia, USA... I didn't see my grandparents, they weren't around.

I was the tenth child of my parents, a happy solemn faced little girl with memories... as far back as four years old......oh, but the thought of yesterday sometimes escapes me.

We ate breakfast, lunch, and dinner in the kitchen separated from the actual house setting. One evening... at about age four, near six o'clock p.m., after eating dinner, I was wrapped in a cover over my head. I looked like a hooded knight, the weather was cold, and I recall my mother calling to my siblings, "Where the baby?"...I was being transported by one of my siblings to the residential setting apart from the kitchen. And I appeared from under the hood of cloth, into a world... that I remember well, to say ..."Here I am."

* *

Many things transpired at four years old, that I remember. Marriage(s) in my family, the old doll house, playing under the shade tree, scenes all pleasantly vivid in my life. I grew happier everyday, solemn faced but... happy. I was a very happy child, with the... days of mud pies, and playing house keeper, and the perfect imitation of a very, would be schoolteacher. One of my desires was to..... teach school, I practiced on fellow students even to the likes of the last day of school. At home on the last day of school the fellow students just so happened to be cousins, and my many friends, that agreed with me for a very short instance.....to take paper and pencil in their hands. I love these people today....and I loved teaching them then.....with a passion.

As I grew older at about six years old, I was allowed to carry a small pail of water that .... derived from an old syrup bucket, then empty. In those days it was a usual thing, to start off with a little bucket, of course by the time I was about seven or eight the little syrup bucket got exchanged for a larger pail...with a larger handle than the small pail prior to that had.

Names of people or products are not important in this phase of my life. At five years old, my older siblings took me to school to be in the spelling bee contests, in their eight-grade class. At five years old, no kindergarten was available. I loved spelling with a passion .... and being the winner at contest times. I loved life and friends.

* *

At my age now, 53 years old, I could really summarize my life; married at fifteen, widow at age nineteen, after only four years and two months of marriage, but I will tell you briefly, in short story form, expressing...reminiscing.

At four years old I remember well my state of being, my hopes. I was a little put down.... girl, yet, in my own little mind and world. I... fought for my integrity as the larger beings... thought to intimidate me. I held fast to hope.

With kindheartedness of my dear mother I have felt, dealt with pain and heartache. It ... was to people's advantage to think of kindness as a weakness. I got through, every storm of their imaginations, I fought it, with kindness.

My parents were good to me, they reared me strictly by their standards and values, but well. People would yell at me just to see my reaction, of which was very scary to me. After all, I was only four years old. I had my own world to.... deal with, I took pride in friendships, even at an early age. I thought deep ...then....and now.

I tried to be good, so I didn't have to get yelled at. I'd say..."Don't be bad or they'll yell at you," but I always, stumbled onto something that I got spanked for...no matter how hard I tried. At four, I'd sit for hours in the sun, writing on the ground, mostly drawing pictures of houses with windows, and curtains. The steps, to the houses were short, so you could get there quicker. I'd draw trees along with grass...how nice to just draw in ease... in my little world.

* *

In a little world with big people it sometimes is a cause for concern. My little world, which would one day result to be printed in a book... my book...but little did I know then as I wrote on the ground that the Strong Being that I felt watching over me would be manifested in a.... book on a page. A Wonderful Friend.....God.

Now I know it was God. I could feel the power of His Being pressing gently upon my life my being, I was lost in Him and in scribbling in... the sand or any surface for drawing or writing.

The feeling was a good one, there I was a little girl, as I squatted on the ground drawing, not knowing that I was being blessed by the very.... Hand of God,now I know. At five years old things took a turn in my artistic behaviors, I started to write two words.Taught by a girl named Mildred, I learned "My First Spelling Words"of which will be printed in this book. I don't know the reason I wasn't taught the words dog, cat, apple or ball... but, I distinctly remember these two words. By the way you will discover the two words in the above stated poem to be "mother" and " father."

I remember reading the book*"Growing Up and Liking It",* a book on puberty and it was snatched from my five year old hands and mind by my mom. I read about the sperm and the egg...whatever that was suppose to mean to my five year old mentality...but I read it with glee...I loved to read. My dad used to say "She goes to bed with a book, and get up with one." I would fall asleep reading, upon awakening I got started again...passionately.

* *

I played with my dolls, taught them school, and then it was my turn to go into a world I would never forget and it was the first grade at six years old. My first day at school wasn't too marvelous either, I got sick the first part of the day at lunch due to a dish of macaroni and cheese.Tell me the reason that I'd get sick from macaroni and cheese? Less fortunate and was not used to such dish. I was mostly used to fat back, biscuits, gravy, turnip greens, vegetables but not....macaroni and cheese. I didn't eat that food dish again until I turned the age twenty-five ...I guess I had to acquire the taste.

At age five, nearly six I was bitten by a black widow spider as I carried cabbage leaves obediently in my dress tail....as per my mother's request. I was struck by the black widow spider's bite in about four places on my inside thigh. I almost died from that unfortunate accident, but due to a neighbor's quick knowledge I survived. She immediately requested that I be taken from the cart in the front yard, and phoned for help.

I attempted to walk when I was tested, on my way to the rescue squad approximately ...a few miles away. I was lowered to the ground, to see if I could walk,I slowly collapsed to the ground. They caught me just before I reached the surface, and then trod onward to the precise pick up point. At the time they used a specific landmark to find the ailing patrons on the county's rural routes. As the rescue squad crew arrived I heard the siren twice then..... I blacked out.

* *

After being in an unconscious state for six days I came to the awakening of a six day ordeal that I was not aware of. They pumped my stomach and did all else to save my life, I'm thankful today for God's miracle to me.

From the ages seven to ten years old it was routinely the same. School, homework, play and chores. I then moved on to the brilliant... teenage years. First date came about at age fifteen, it took place at the county fair, it was fun.

After some courtship I did a teenage mistake becoming pregnant, married at fifteen, widow at nineteen...and single parent of two children.

Now, here we are back to the point which I summarized my life. Now life is great and it is sweet, but it brings along with it, many facets of failure and promises.

At nineteen, I was a runaway child, running wildly about. Doing my own thing took me to the state of Pa., USA. I was in a not so pleasant situation. I'm just thankful that I'm one of the battered women that got out in time....a bonus.

This book is not about sadness or negatives... but about hope and achievement of our dreams. So from that note, I move on with a smile and a greatness of character and integrity. I went to a many job sites and searches, I ended up with the Feds, in the latter sense of the matter.

I remarried thirty-two years later after being single that long, but not before, eighteen years of deep devotion to God, which, still goes forth today, with the richness of His love in my life.

* *

I thank God for the fervent hope and eternal life promised to me by His Word and His Spirit the Holy Ghost that I received in 1983, after being baptized in Jesus name by the pastor and... other clergy of my church.

This brings me to the present time in my life all else will be expressed in poetry as everyday life like situations. I really call them ..."times and situations in life." God is in control and I do accept things in my life in victory but not in defeat. For I will never be defeated if I keep my hands in God's Hand.... my heart in His Word.

I hope that you've at least enjoyed the wholesome shortness of my life's story. One day in details I just may submit it in writing, but until then come along on this journey of...friendship.

I've had a many friends and yet have many,... and with God's help I'll be there for them.Only believe that I have feelings.... just like everyone else. Only believe that this is my story of my life and many of you have inspired me to write thus ...and I thank God for you.

To put in a serious note I will discuss the job with the Feds. On the job with the Feds, I went through a hard hearted show of hands. If you want my presence, speaking of the Feds, let me know, it went on for years. Everyday I learned something about them and myself. My work... spoke for itself, yet harassed sometimes daily. My production spoke for itself, until I got hurt by lifting a cart stuck in an elevator crevice.... loaded with documents, thereby causing injury.

* *

After, hurting my back, right there on the... job I've had unimaginable pain. From... that day on, the real fight was on. Harassed about what I can, and cannot perform. Through therapy, outside doctors, and bedrest at the on the job health station, and pain medications that I couldn't administer at work... I managed barely to grit my teeth for seven years, two months.

It was a long time to try to work being in pain after the on- the-job back injury, before resigning in complete exhaustion and severe, extreme pain in the lower back, and radiation to the lower extremities. At last some compassion, I think not, but at least some compensation for my faithful service to the Feds, whilst I was on the workroom floor. The case is still pending, the result of my suffering from the injury, remains today.

Now for a happier note...let's continue on to another challenge of ideas. Remain encouraged. It's tough to unlearn what you've learned if you don't use force and persistence.The enemy is not going to just let you walk around in ease...it's a daily fight. Get ready for the war against negatives, and ...enter in peace, with your fellowman.

By encouraging others, you encourage yourself, by elevating others, you elevate yourself. Be good to others, and be good to yourself. Now that the preliminaries are over, and the case at hand is to encourage people let's get up to a higher mountain of hope. Let's reach ...so high into the realm of faith that the present suffering and discomfort is only but... for a moment, or seem that way.

* *

Be it to teach, or to reach someone, let's do it all to the Glory of God! All "one day at a time," we can build character in ourselves, and others, if only we'd be compassionate...not hating the person, but the aspect of their adverse actions.

People are good all over the world, let's show love across the board and everything else will fall in place. I love the Lord, my fellowman and I love life in the Lord. I hope that this stay was pleasant to you, now let's move on with integrity of heart, and compassion at your fingertips.

I was reared by my parents in respect, dignity, and faith in God. I wasn't given an option to... have self-pity, these people meant to rear us to be fit for the world's toughness, survival of the fittest with....hopes of becoming proud parents.

Enjoy the richness of diversity in your life and whilst you're at it, add a little spice to someone else's life.....someday they may thank you for it.

You will forever have...*"The Ring Of Friends: Forever" Poem Collection* as a reminder that .... your friend was once a stranger to you, but now you've met and happy are you. Following this... page, I will add poetry of my childhood lessons:

"My First Spelling Words"
"Mother, You've Taught Me A Lot"
"Father, I Have Learned From You"
"The Salt Substitute"
"My Children" & "Strength Be There For Me"
"Don't Try To Help Me, You Already Have"

* *

* *

" My First Spelling Words "

My first spelling words were, "Mother" and "Father," a girl named, Mildred started me on my way,
When I was five years old, and loved to just scribble, Mildred taught me one day.
She said, sit here and she began to teach me the words, "Mother" and "Father,"
She didn't have to take the time to do that, neither did she have to bother.
I'm thankful today as I remember, and it has taken me through things in my life at best,
I often wonder today, had the first two words not been, "Mother" and "Father," would I have passed the test.
I pressed my way to perfection, and I didn't forget where I came from long ago,
And I say to Mildred, I remember "My First Spelling Words," being "Mother" and "Father" and... I wanted you to know.
Thanks, Mildred, you taught me a foundation ...and I remember you,
You taught me two important words, and may God bless you in all that you do.
For "My First Spelling Words," " Mother" and "Father," are still present right now with me,
And I reminisce over old times, for it was vivid enough for me to see.
With "My First Spelling Words" ... "Mother" and "Father" the dreams... live on.

* *

" Mother, You Have Taught Me A Lot "

"Mother, You Have Taught Me A Lot" by your caring ways,
You have pressed your way to help others even, through endless days.

You have taught me love when people didn't love me back,
No matter how they treated you, you gave them no slack.

You have taught me to serve others when they needed it most,
Then you taught me to ride off into the sunset, and not boast.

Through your strong constitution, and your very steadfast faith in the Master's love,
You have taught me to above all, look to God up above.

You taught me courage, to take life on with all I could possibly do,
Even, the poetry all started with a gift from God, and the encouragement, while young ... from you.

Mother, the things you've taught me, I have not forgot,
It takes me a long way now, and "Mother, You Have Taught Me A Lot."

* *

" Father, I Have Learned From You "

"Father, I Have Learned From You,"that to be dignified, respectful, and holding up the family name,
Would all one day come as a blessing to me, and equal out the same.

You talked to me, and taught me about love, and patience too,
For you wanted me to know the hard knocks of life, and be just like you.

You carried yourself with respect, status and pride,
You did your part to take care of us, and you didn't just go along for the ride.

When we got ourself into a mess and needed you to help us out,
You often would tell us before you helped ... it's your red wagon, so don't you pout.

You taught me that no matter what... business and friendship do not mix,
And that, what you didn't start with you didn't have to fix.

So I take heed, to all you have said to me, and all you wanted me to do,
Now, I can say to it all,"Father, I Have Learned From You."

* *

" The Salt Substitute "

When I was raised I was taught a lot of things to do,
If we didn't have one thing, we were taught to do without it too.
So my parents taught me, that if I didn't have one thing, to use something else instead,
As, I was taught if I didn't have cornmeal, use the flour for bread.
So it stuck in my head as they said, the world owe you nothing at all,
So I was told to use pepper when I didn't have salt... and think it not small.

As I grew older I pondered in my mind, that... how could pepper, be a substitute for salt,
But when I didn't substitute things, and do without, it ended up my fault.
So as I go about life, I try to follow my parent's lead,
I use the old adage "The Salt Substitute" indeed.
Now when I don't have salt, then pepper would be the thing,
And when I hear people say, we don't have salt, I hear a familiar ring.

My parent's voices echoes to me, and help me even today,
So, I don't feel sorry for myself, then "self-pity" .... had to go away.

* *

" My Children "

**All the world in the many generations at best,
Can really help each other to truly pass the test.
We can face hurdles of life and be on our way,
All we do in this world, and lifetime will help our memories stay.
Yet when it comes to our children we shelter, and soften things for them too,
It may not be a bad idea, to allow them to have something to do.
Children surprisingly know sometimes what they need for themselves,
So why don't we give them space to grow up, and not put advice back on the shelves.
Every family is different in their unique way,
And I cherish my children, and the generation of people, as I pray.
Keeping also "My Children" encouraged, and it's truly a blessing to me,
For all I know sometimes.... " My Children " help me to see.**

" Strength Be There For Me "

**Strength be there for me when I really need you the most,
When all is said and done let us of the Lord truly boast.
We try to be very content, prosperous and strong willed,
Yet we are but men, and by the hand of God can be made still.
Still in our endeavors our situations too, We can help others along the way more than we do. As I look for a friendly hello and there's none for me to see, ...Strength, I need your encouragement, so " Strength Be There For Me."**

* *

" Don't Try To Help Me, You Already Have "

(Part I)

I've searched for encouragement but you gave me a hard time,
I searched for a beyond the job life when I did not have a dime.
You left me and ridiculed me, you left me.... alone you see,
The times were tough, being my sorrows were born in me.
I asked for your help and kind understanding you refused,
I rushed to my feet to laugh again, and be self amused.
You passed up my feelings,treated me real bad,
You talked about me and the trials that I had.
You told me in so many words to just go away,
I walked away in tears, and because of your wishes, I didn't stay.
All in all I struggled, I toiled and daily I strive to be me,
And at last I came to my senses, and I was free.
I became free as a bird let out of a snare,
All because you didn't reach out to help me, and be there.
Somehow the strength I got from the lack of care,
Placed my feet on the road across from despair.
I was built up in my character, by selfish actions you had,
And I waited at last, thoughts being free, not sad.
Because you didn't reach with outstretched arms,
I've gotten to my feet and have braved the storms.

* *

" Don't Try To Help Me, You Already Have"

(Part II)

I now can really look back over my dear life,
To see clearly the turmoil, clearly the strife.
The harmony that I've acquired of my test,
The seemingly harm helped me to do my best.
Of all that I've learned from friends at hand,
Is that, through all the lack of encouragement,
I still had to stand.
I stood to my feet with my head lifted up high,
I looked to my friends as they blessedly went by.
As a relief from my troubles, and breather for
time being,
I searched my way, to what I really was seeing.
I looked and I saw, that you had unknowingly
helped me,
For when you refused to help me, my strength
came to be.
You came to me now after I've come through
my trials, you desperately want now to help me
out with some smiles.
You made me stronger, by your lack of comfort,
the very opposite of an anointing salve,
So please "Don't Try To Help Me, You Already
Have."
I can tell others now as they too cry out for help,
That I too have been through lack of friends,
and how I've wept.
So through all that life offers, no need keeping
the tab, and I say to you, "Don't Try To Help
Me, You Already Have."

Building friendships everyday is an ordeal... that calls for patience, longsuffering, growth... every direction of positiveness prospers greatly.

We want for a special time and essence of love to fulfil our dreams and hopes.... in *"The Ring Of Friends: Forever"*.... love never stop flowing.

After rejoicing with family, coworkers, friends for years on end, we feel enriched by the character it bestows upon our being. As we let the continuos flow of friendship bring us to a rescued state of longing for peace and solitude.....we're relaxed, and in a calm presence of love.

When we touch the love of friends, it causes an effect upon us that need no help with pressing it upon our minds.....for it's stable and well able to subdue hardships and pain.

"The Ring Of Friends: Forever" brings you... closer to God, loved ones, friends, and will in a positive way touch your heart and mind by.... its words of wisdom and strength.

As you read on in a joyous state, stay encouraged in life, and ever blessed by God.....for He awaits your cry and praise of honest integrity.

When life offers us friends....we need to reach out and accept it as God sends it our way.Things will always work in our favor with gratitude and acceptance of God's will.

Reading with knowledge and understanding.... means more than writing with a sense of satisfaction, for words have more meaning to individuals in solitude at times....than a group of roundtable patrons at heart.This book is for people in search of solitude and peace, where love flows....peace is found. May you find it in family as well as friends.

When we read we want an uplifting to take place as it fares well in our life when it has the right zing and lift. Presently, as we read poetry it has its rhyme, flow, and heartfelt phrases to ease the pains and downtrends in life.

There are many books and poets, yet let this book be a companion to your feelings and set it alongside for your reading pleasures...and feel better about life and love. Windows of good.... things will open for you as you venture out into a pleasant world of poetry......as read by many happier people.

We all want to come to a solemn and precise conclusion when searching for happiness. Let it be found in God and your heart, for then it will venture to great things and beyond.

By now you've experienced many verses also phrases, and rhymes...pass it along to a friend. Let it ever be a treasure in your heart and mind as read in intellectual stages of hope and uplifting serenity to all people and in all walks of life.

We will spend a lot of our waking hours encouraging friends to go the extra length in life. Reminiscing about issues in our lives seem to.. be the conversation in latter times.

Encouragement is sought seemingly daily yet we find it in few friends. Trustworthy friends.. that stand to reason in our favor are deeply.... searched for.

Whether we ever reach the goals in obtaining friendship, we will have at least tried if we will but...show ourselves friendly. Search again..... and again. It is great to be amongst friends in the midst of blue skies and a handful of hope.

* *

Poems...

For Busy People....

For Tired People...

For Friends.........

When you can't be everything...just be you

Sometimes we need to take a break from it all... and grasp enthusiasm on our way, then we are greatly strengthened everyday....Pausing...... Moving....in Transit......Delivered....with a... Smile.

Knowingly, God has in store for you, what's for you.....and it will be in the final analysis yours.

Fretting over changes in life will not outlive hope...only hope can outlive hope.

During lifetime the course must be ran, whether with family and friends by your side..... yet run on. After all is said and done you will solemnly know that you stood firm, believing God, family, friends, but at least..... you believed in yourself......when at times, no one other than God did.

* *

" When I Was Four "

A brilliant cloud appeared one day upon
my door, as I awakened, as I slept as before.
I looked in amazement at the silhouette that
I saw before me,
As I screamed over the top of my voice, at
what I did see.
It was for my comfort for it did not offend,
and now for many years I see it in the end.
I recognize that it meant something very
dear to me, for insight of events beforehand
now come to be.
I enjoy the wisdom that it bestows upon my
being, for after all these years, I can believe
...what I'm seeing.

" A Twelve Year Old "

The mind is young and mixed, all lined in a
row, a lot of things these youngsters do not
know.
Yet they press their way onward to goals at
last, things seem to be traveling for them so
very fast.
There's hope for them of becoming the......
famous thirteen, and then they will really
know what a teenager mean.

* *

" Put Me In Your Circle "

This is where I'll stay all the while you're near, for you've been a dear friend, one who really hear.
To hear my beck and call when my spirit is not at a high,
To hear my heart speak out for love as life goes slowly by.
As you speak things into existence of all the hope you'd find,
I love to be near your caring spirit and... hear your positive mind.

" If I Wrote A Novel "

The novel would be filled with pleasant things you'd love to hear,
Resting quietly and reading words so very near.
It would explain life, and how you can make it, it also would tell you how you can take it.
It would let you see that things are yet grand, as you stay in the race and ever make your stand.
Now we've heard enough of the sad times and recession,
"If I Wrote A Novel" I'd make a glorious impression.

* *

" Best Things "

Being in God and free, being you and me.
Being of a glorious kind, being in our...
right mind.
"Best Things" could always be, "Best
Things" in you and me.
Feeling victorious everyday, feeling at
ease if you may.
All the "Best Things" in life can never
suffice, perfect love and great sacrifice.
"Best Things" when Jesus died for us all,
that we may live,
"Best Things" to our fellowman like love
we can give.

"Fresh Cut Blossoms"

Where and why they were picked matters
not, just a closeness of feelings not soon
forgot.
The look of the stems that hold the flowers,
will ever hold your attention even until the
hour.
Flowers are daily held in hope of a patron's
request, as the "Fresh Cut Blossoms" ......
withstand its test.
They try not to wither and fade away, as...
thoughtful wishes come on today.
Buy some for your loved ones, family and
friend, let the happiness of your caring ways
begin.

* *

" Landscape "

Tree are set by a handy man's wisdom. The sun shows its brilliance upon flowers and greenery.
Birds chirp gracefully upon a well kept lawn, and camera sounds brings joy to my heart.

" Your Job "

It's yours they say when you're at work, doing the best you can do,
You help out in a team spirit doing your duty, and sometimes more too.
Yet, when you're away from the workplace for whatever the reason,
Then it's no longer "Your Job" until you return in any given season.

" My Job "

I'm working now, so that I don't have to work in a future time,
To save for retirement or not to save has its own rhyme.
I say sometimes that I can't afford to save or do such a thing,
Yet, it's the opposite...I really can't afford not to save, as it in my mind ring. So I do without it now, and have it in days of ease…then I can go cruising, live in Florida, or do as I please.

* *

“ Victory Over Obstacles ”

Moments in our life will come that cause concern,
We must go on, and press over trials as we learn.
It won’t help to allow the negatives to come in,
Don’t even think on it, but with your mind, do defend.
Be a defender of the hopes in your very life,
Strive to be victorious, and overcome strife.
On every hand many obstacles are laid in our way,
As we speak “Victory Over Obstacles”…on every day.

“ Help Someone Else To See Their Way ”

You’ve been there, done that many times over, it was tough through life, not a bed of clover.
Let them know you’ve been a forerunner all along, it will help them to believe and keep them strong.
If others that progress can make it okay,
You also can do the same thing everyday.
So learn from other people’s experiences and save yourself the pain,
“Help Someone Else To See Their Way” …... and let it their gain.

* *

" Remind Yourself "

"Remind Yourself " that you know what to do, you've been grown for a while now, as others too.
Why aggravate yourself with things of grief,
When you can face it straight up and get some relief.
You don't have to accept circumstances as they are, change what you can and stay up to par.
So "Remind Yourself " that you're somebody tough, and with God's help it won't seem so rough.

" A Child's Prayer "

(Poem I)

Lord bless me as I leave home for school,
For I'm going everyday to learn the golden rule.
It will help me grow along the way, and I will graduate when I can no longer stay.
You wake me up upon every morn, You've blessed me every since I was born.

" A Child's Prayer "

(Poem II)

God bless my Mom, also bless my Dad,
Wonderful parents that anyone ever had.
Help me to make them proud as can be,
That they may both see themselves in me.

* *

" On Top Of The City Building "

Somehow someone thought to put my beauty
hereabout,
A touch of greenery with blossoms to remove
all doubt.
The featured economy with buildings so tall,
A wonder of plants also set in array in the halls.
I'm a tree that's planted " On Top Of The City
Building " for a view,
So please look up in life or I will only be seen...
by a few.

" A Mother's Prayer "

Lord, take all things upon You, help me to
get all the way through.
When I have trials and are at a low, remind
me of the goodness I sow.
Also remind me that You will make a way,
and help me to love people and always pray.

" A Father's Prayer "

Bless me Lord in all that I do, help me to help
others to follow through.
When I look to tomorrow with a smile, keep
me humble and help me over the mile.
I put all things in Your hand to hold, for then
I can go through life's trials feeling bold.

* *

" Grandmother's Love "

Why do you love me so, the answers are not all with me,
For you long to help me out so that my mind will remain free.
Now where can I go and be in a special place, as with you,
A Special Lady, as a "Grandmother's Love" shines through.
Your words comfort my heart and put a smile on my face,
Your touch erases doubt and sends me to a higher place.

" Grandfather's Love "

No question of your love for you show it... on everyday,
It's mostly in your deeds and the kind... words you say.
You press upon my mind to live happily... and free,
And that places a firm and steady glow... upon me.
You gently guide me as you talk with... wisdom and love,
Then you show me how to live with the... peacefulness of a dove.

* *

" Our Relationship "

The Spring, brings about a freshness of flow-
ers upon our love, gently flowing and with
the essence of Our Father up above.
The Summer, brings a hope that we need after
the flowers peek, rushing upon our dearest
hearts as we each other seek.
The Autumn, brings a color that burst upon
the fresh air, enhancing the quality of our love
that we do wholesomely share.
The Winter, brings a warmth that we spread
to each other in love, and "Our Relationship"
was sent from.....Our Dear Father up above.

" There's A Friend Somewhere "

There has to be a friend, if we'd search at will,
That will encourage us, and also help us still.
There has to be a friend that we can really trust,
That will help us get the job done when we must.
There has to be a friend, at least one in this wide
world as a whole, that will help fulfill our wishes,
dreams and be bold.
There has to be a friend in the city, the country...
or in a land far or near, that will also hold your
friendship as meaningful and dear.
"There's A Friend Somewhere" search for them
and seek them out, and remember to keep the
ring of friends, that your life has brought about.

* *

" No Magical Time For Education "

**Let it fare better to get the benefit of school
at youth,
Jobs has more availability and we learn it's
the truth.
It's a continuous thing even after high school
is done,
A great thing to do after you realize upon the
rising sun.
If returning to school is of your great desire,
Complete your course, your friend will admire.
Even though you accomplish it in such a short
frame, you won't really be feeling the same.
So remember there's "No Magical Time For
Education" to appear,
So press forward to your marvelous graduation,
that's so dear.**

" Spread The Word Of Cheer "

**Pick it up please and pass it on, for the need is
always there,
Hoping, helping, caring, and many nice things
to share.
If, in fact you feel better from just reading a
poem or two,
Send the vibes charging peacefully on, get the
dear word through.
Let people know there's hope and share info
if you can,
"Spread The Word Of Cheer" for nowadays it
has its demand.**

* *

" Don't Put It Off "

**If you're not around a lot of friends it's okay,
There's no real challenge, they're here to stay.
We'd get along just fine as we're used to doing,
Yet it would be great if friends we're pursuing.**

**If you don't have any, seem it better for you,
All you have to do is make yourself friendly too.
Then the world of friends will open up….. and there they will be,
" Don't Put It Off " for the fellowship is something you can see.**

**You see it right in your daily walk as you arise,
Strength you receive just might be a surprise.
Strength in unity, strength in the smiles galore,
Try it for yourself… you'll see what's in store.**

" Now What Are You Going To Do? "

**You've reached a peak in your life, satisfied and feeling free,
Yet, let not the focus be all on self and leave out dear me.
It would be a blessing just touch a life or two, for what you share with family and friends… keeps them from feeling blue.
Just a word of hope, add some gladness in your daily walk too,
You know the answer……"Now What Are You Going To Do?"**

* *

" Readers, Writers, Critics and Friends "

**Well read, well written, critics on corners,
friends at hand,
Marvelously all in place to capture all the
moments that you stand.
Be it ever a gratitude of best times all in
good taste,
For the "Readers, Writers, Critics and
Friends" you won't want to waste.
I guess you know they will help you along,
So why be concerned with all that's said,
for they will make you strong.**

" The Gathering "

**People will be strong and feel the flow
of your love,
Pressing onward to freedom and peace
as of a dove.
When time permits them to, they will
check on you,
A few words, a few smiles, will certainly
channel through.
What would be the best time to meet and
greet a friend,
Would it even fare better to just press it
to the end.
For hope is found in peaceful words, or
just a chosen few,
Try "The Gathering," enjoy your family,
friends, and begin a friendship anew.**

* *

" Meaning Of Life "

Purpose, fulfillment, God's way and will,
wholesomely impressed upon all of us still.
Youthful days of hope, solemn faces of ....
destination,
Pressing love upon our hearts and minds of
God's manifestation.
When love is flowing freely, who can really
be left out,
When we press upon our minds leaving out
all doubt.
Be it great to visit a person or just leave it be,
Is in the "Meaning Of Life" for us all to see.
God has a purpose for us He knows best,
"Meaning Of Life"...is richly in every test.

" The Secret Closet "

Want to reach out to friends, family and
fellowman,
Taking some things lightly, when we don't
understand.
Want to reach out to neighbors, coworkers
if that is the norm,
Taking things for granted, like the passing
of the thunderstorm.
Want to bring reality closer to your life in
view of God's blessing,
Find "The Secret Closet," meet Him, and
find a place of resting.

* *

" When The World Wants More, Give It To God "

Of all the demands that life has pressed upon your door, some will be a little lighter if God's will you adore.
We grow up and feel the world at our back,
Pressing upon our character singling out lack.
Once the lack is defined whether it's joy or peace of mind, you will see the world release an attitude of a different kind.
God's Word is powerful, reaching mountains and the valley, and " When The World Wants More, Give It To God" for He'll keep the tally.

" Hardship Or Friendship "

Let's just say when hard knocks of life come we can be strong with a smile, for the hope that is reached will be present all the while.
We don't always experience the cushion of things that comes along, sometimes we feel the rigid bumps, when thought wrong.
Let's just say take it and stride along in life's victories, for without pain we wouldn't reach the presence of peaceful seas.
Let's say we reach out to faith in God and then we believe, let's say during " Hardship Or Friendship " we reach to God and receive.
For He meets us whatever the hour in our dearest concern, let's say "Hardship Or Friendship" releases God's love as we learn.

* *

" Closer "

The awesome presence of God flowing freely, releasing hope, touching love, erasing doubt, pressing forth.
Quietly and powerful, and every moment a precious rose resteth upon our hearts. Petals fully bursting in mercy and grace, thoughts come forth of Saints, reminiscing of a better place.

" The Fervent Presence Of God "

The session of daytime does not always permit the peacefulness, the quietness.
Busy times, workdays, family and friends are advanced with demands.
Oh, the precious moments have now arrived, the birds won't tweet, the phone won't ring, quietness is felt, power is full, prayer is going up...we're in "The Fervent Presence Of God."

" The Grace Of God "

Oh, what sweet relief and peacefulness from the freedom of pain, when oftentimes we pray and it yet remains. It's not because God is not able to remove it, for He's well able even if He doesn't prove it. But be thankful for His power is real, rest in Him, wait and He will heal. Moment by moment, and hour by hour, feel "The Grace Of God " for He has the power.

* *

" When We Touch God "

Where would one find the quietness of nature had it not been for God. The more we reach to Him, He presses a flow of love upon our hearts. Glorious ways, feelings, emotions run like a ... river of water upon our soul.
Love presses forth to serve Him, resting in His mercy and grace, we receive a fellowship to worship Him.
Deep goes the heart and mind, love flows.... freely, words are at a pace of praise.
Our face shine boldly, hearts feel lighter, our soul is cleansed...... "When We Touch God."

" Pressing On "

Going past concerns in life, press to achieve, past doubts in life, press to believe, past storms, press toward the rainbow, past struggles, press on to know, past tests, trials, press to faith as heard, past negatives, press toward God's Word. Enthusiasm is at hand, as we're "Pressing On" past troubles in the land.

" If You Find "

If you find yourself believing check the belief, relieving check the relief, receiving check the receipt, decreasing then check the decrease, increasing check the source, departing check the destination, friendless check the list, find yourself concerned check faith......and insist.

* *

" The Uplift Of A Friend "

You want to be uplifted, seek a friend, you
want to be enthused, try one to win.
Days will be brighter, nights will have a...
colorful touch, all lives will be touched with
"The Uplift Of A Friend" as such.
For they will then bring your spirits to a high,
It's needed daily, and is marvelous, by and by.
Get " The Uplift Of A Friend " in a daily walk,
have happiness in your daily talk. Get natural
friends, spiritual friends too, let it be the...
" The Uplift Of A Friend "....in you.

" Calendar "

For the seasons we have four, months we have
twelve, days we have many, hours we have ...
twenty-four, minutes we have more.........if we
embrace every hour with love, peace, harmony
of character and hold hands with...God.

When we walk hand in hand with friends we...
have a peaceful resolve, twelve months on the
list it will take friends to get us through, given
by the Hands of God you can...only win.

Wishing blessings upon this home all year long.
Hope for hearts, integrity for our minds. Joy in
our voice, and love in our actions.
Once upon a time of freedom let it ring upon our
heart, friendship, let it be from the start. Twelve
months to grow stronger...in love and grace.

The hope of seeing and visiting friends are... narrowly perceived at times as being bothersome. Once we press past the obstacles of time frames we will have enjoyed a lifetime of wealth.

Why not take the challenge of blessed hope by discussions of life in general, as you read along and enjoy this book of poems.

Releasing the pressures of daily living and fulfilling your dreams with peace and harmony, at its best is done amongst friends. Who but needs a friend as nowadays, when society is in an uproar and life flashes reality before us. It's all accounted to our good if we...reach out to sincere friends sent from God.

It's the dawn of a new day when people envision the need for comfort from friends.Of course, many obstacles will appear and ....must be overcome by love and understanding.

Treating friends as family and the chosen few coworkers on secular jobs as family fares well in this Millennium era. When is a visit to friends a necessity or.... wanting of integrity drives home some important points...you decide.

There is no magical moment to adhere to or a solemn advance to traditional rights in our mind. We must follow our hearts in order to reach a.... peaceful state of being during these trying times. We can not depend mostly on friends, but God... first of all in all of our endeavors.

When we revisit our friends it brings about a hope rekindled, youthful talks revived, and a.... wholesome character.

It must be fervent in one's mind the heart-felt need to administer the oneness of friends, before one can be turned in either direction to visit or not to visit.

A visit to friends is not a stay but a whole-some intellectual part of rebuilding friendship, all one step at a time. To revisit friends brings us one-step further to the convenience of being in the company of warmth, and caring mature adults. Revisit friends today and let happiness unfold...in many ways.

Conversing over a cup of coffee or tea...fares well with friends, for it brings about a warmth of ideas, and a long sought after victory, that... have now come to pass.

A nice breakfast, lunch, dinner...then a walk, kicking a few rocks along the way as your friend-ship lingers long and heartily upon the beach.... or other selected place of harmony and peace, also fares well.

Eventually you will encounter people in all.... walks of life, yet revisiting friends brings about a sense of hope, of returning again to....rekindle and rebuild. It's as if a fireplace is in need of the natural hand of man to restart its flame.

All too well we sometimes need a reminder of how wonderful life really is...God first and then friends...will do just that.

We all have a sense of direction, whether to our liking or someone else's. We would like to think that the direction that we choose will be pleasing... to Almighty God.

* *

" School Days "

With friends at every hand we're more happy today,
Calling up a few to see if they're going your way.
Mostly not because they even need the ride,
But it's really a great thing to be with them in stride.
They're a great bunch of people to be in the presence of and learn,
It's all a zing of hope and love to really with them earn.
To earn your way through an education would be the greatest thing,
Especially, after all of the study you finally get your ring.
Then on to another level of college, be it early or late,
You will always remember your friends and " School Days" in your state.

" Don't Read This "

Okay, the thing is not to read this poem,
You're determined as we of the norm.
Why are you this far, you're really brave?
Might as well read one more verse to save.
You've got this far, it said "Don't Read This,"
But that's the way you will get through life, if ...you will insist.

* *

" School Parking "

**Where are all my friends, are they here as yet?
For they have the privilege to have a space all set.
Now it's something that is earned, and friends feel the joy, what an excellent way to enjoy their car as a toy.
Now these are responsible people for their friend keep them in line,
They encourage each other daily, saying you're doing fine.
Then one day the time will come that you will be moving on, someone else will step in just in time when the slot is born.
It's a nice thing to feel grown and wait in line for a place to park,
For it raises the level of reasoning when "School Parking" ...you will embark.**

" Stop Now "

**"Stop Now" the negative bring the positive in line, stop now the unhappiness and your hope will be fine.
"Stop Now" the gloom of life for the sun shines free, stop now the not so pleasant things that come to be.
"Stop Now" the disappointment, roll on to another verse, it goes to show that you have incentives or it could have been worse.**

* *

" On the Court "

Dribble the ball, slam dunk it in place,
Keeping peace with friends in this race.
To be strong with feelings of encourage-ment to spread out,
Planning a shot on the floor, making a score no doubt.
What a feeling it is to be together again to bond,
Making all the difference as you're .... complacently fond.
It's good to share your youthful days at hand, for when you're older you will... remember it in your stand.
It's a youthful thing that's earned and of a different sort,
When you're feeling free with friends, you enjoy being "On the Court."

" You Will "

Why do people say you won't when... really by faith.... "You will?"
Put you down when you're really up?
Try to do you harm, but you're calm?
People seem to not know that you'll go?
That you won't grow, but you show?
Say that you're late, not knowing fate?
You never will, yet you're over the hill?
Why they talk "you won't," when you're positively walking ...."You Will."

* *

" At The Movies "

Whether the screen is close or far it's
gain to be involved,
For it's a place to be when you have
situations solved.
It's for relaxation and to share a real
helping hand, making a graceful try at
helping your friend to stand.
Call them up and make a plan for the
best time frame,
Expressly following through when you
are feeling the same.
To share life together and then to really
know your ways,
Will all be great for friendship, and it's
the way it stays.
Your friends may travel to a far land
one day and then you will part,
Yet the time that you all spent "At The
Movies"...will remain in your heart.

" If You Don't "

"If You Don't" press...you won't succeed,
Don't rest.....you won't have time to read.
No time to read.... what will you do? Had
time to read you'd get through. Don't set
priorities, time will then slip away. Don't
push forward, how can you stay? Don't
use what you've got....will it then be lost?
Don't write poems.....how will you know
you're ...not a Robert Frost?

* *

" A Happy Teacher "

**The express job of the teaching world
is to be an example,
Children come from all over the world
to just give a sample.
It would fare better to tell them to be-
have and to get ahead,
If they would only listen to the teacher
it would not be a dread.
How do the students then have the time
to play around in the class,
When the teacher will have lessons
that will in their lifetime last.**

**Be it everyday or every time they get a
chance to be at the top of the line,
It will be the best thing for them to be
gentle and kind.
It's a marvelous idea for them to sit and
adhere to the rules of the game,
For the teaching from all teachers will
not really be the same.
Some students will learn and go on their
way to a better day,
Some will just sit there as if they're not
motivated in any way.**

**Whatever you teach them they will let you
know if it's a success,
For if you want to be "A Happy Teacher"
you must keep them at their best.**

* *

" For Teacher "

You teach me ABC's, you teach me how
to bend, and then reach to my knees.
You teach me P's and Q's, you teach me
how to tie a bow on my pair of shoes.
You teach me the colors of my crayons,
You teach me how to make my rounds.
You teach me how to wait my own turn,
You teach me and I do try to daily learn.
You teach me of a strong church's chapel,
You teach me well, I bring you an apple.
You teach me how to become very bright,
You teach me how to read and also write.
And now you teach me what I need to say,
I might want to be a teacher also one day.
People will learn my ways....good or bad,
So I learn from all the teaching I've had.
Thank You Teacher.........For all you do.

" Wishing Well "

Golden depth upon the well, for all the
people do tell.
They come from far and near, just to cast
a wish to bear.
They cast their wish upon the air, where it
goes we know not where.
Yet we do believe that our wish come true,
wishing nice things for me and you.
So make a wish and toss your coin, and see
your wish come true upon the morn.

* *

" A Fond Weekend "

Draped in a state of need for the fresh air
is here,
When the workweek is over and you cherish
it so dear.
Now you could say that the week was tough
and long,
If you did you might join in the seemingly…
regular chorus song.
For we sing that song especially if we work…
mostly everyday,
Just to make things wonderful to dearly help
us on our way.
It's great to say the job is grand at least it…
helps us out,
That way we can go to work when the clock
lets out a shout.
It says to us get up and go, for it's the thing
for us to do,
So you at other times agree and begin to…
follow through.
Sometimes it is said, " I'm so tired I don't
know what to do,"
Yet, you look forward to "A Fond Weekend"
that the end of the workweek promises you.

" Keeping Pace "

The sounds of the weekend, falls upon ears
with gladness, derived as hope. Let it stay
upon happy notes and bring us to not mope.

* *

"Grateful Speaks The Marigolds Of London"

Sit we here on our porch of solemn....
complacency. As the drenched flowers
of ease are rained upon.
Set besides the hopscotch fellows, the
boroughs of the complacent best.
Drilled in power of the flowers, in a
wonderful rest.
"Grateful Speaks The Marigolds Of
London,"...hasten to our home.

" Country Roads "

"Country Roads" take me to my neighbor,
helping them by doing a favor. Take me to
their house, their love, upon their peace of
a dove.
"Country Roads" take me past the fields and
farm, teach me the way to peace and calm.
There's something about "Country Roads"
that will always be, for they lead us to our
friends...and family.

" On The Edge Of Town "

When going to be with friends, we can look
up and see the calm state of their caring,
All wrapped up in a marvelous personality
of a wholesome summed up sharing.
We didn't have to go far, to be up to par.

* *

" The Cause Of Your Freedom "

The strength of your character came to be, on past the essence of time, as the world went on as free.
It filtered through hopes and ill wills, and gain, even though you fought through the weight loss as it did remain.
Mostly that, but there's another story, of depression, lost in the time capsule of getting to another session.
Fought by the hand of diligent worth, staggering all the while, from whence comes this story of.... eating beef that didn't bring on a smile.
You won that case that they put before your.... logic mind, for the bother of it all, evidence they could not find.
This is just a sample of things you've been....... through in your career, and the partial sadness of the media in the rear.
Oprah, you've advanced to another stage not far from the depths of praise, you've had many of... those lonely nights and many hectic days. But... now, how your spirit have reached so many dear folks, and it was "The Cause Of Your Freedom" and breaking the yolks.

Dedicated to: Ms Oprah Winfrey
07/04/2001 2:18 AM DST
Best Wishes To You, You Make Me Proud

* *

" Recent Findings "

Who would classify the worth of the TV Stations, as being fulfilled, as you can see the hope and the presence of the Lord's Divine will.
It's really an easy thing to adjust in your daily routine to stay, for the Show is hosted for twenty-four hours of every God given day.
It has its way of reaching the far lands as needed throughout, many programs heartfelt, and bringing many to shout.
It's a good cause, and you will agree to the gesture at hand, for it came about by two wonderful people named " Paul & Jan. "
The world would be starved of the good that they could do, if they were not blessed as well, with your donations to "TBN" coming through.
So now we have the " I do pledge an amount " to help the work on "TBN," and the " Recent Findings" of all the Stations has caused them to win. It boosts their morale, and put fellowship in their plan for people to unite, for the whole story of the matter is they do not give up the fight.
Daily the Stations continue to grow and let it be "The Holy Spirit's" Will, for the " Recent Findings " of more Stations On "TBN"....... is going on still.

Dedicated To: Paul & Jan Crouch At TBN 07/04/ 2001 4:40 AM DST
Best Wishes To You, You All Make Me Proud

* *

" Little Friends "

**The names are not really important when
you're having fun,
For the enhancement of life is welcomed in
the sun.
Not very tall or very big but you mean a lot,
to me,
For you tell me that I do well in things I do
not see.**

**You build my character up to the point of
a smile,
And I never knew it would really take me
over the mile.
It's great to be amongst people that we...
share life with today,
For right now we're " Little Friends " but
one day will set a trend to stay.
We will grow up and then we may even...
move away to another town,
But the bond of our friendship will renew
and forever be around.**

" Love "

**Full of joy passed through stages of hope,
left upon the wings of the wind as it blew
in a smile.
The heart is warmed in beauty, the mind
is fed of action, and the dreams of life are
fully attended to...by kindness and grace.**

* *

" A Grown-up Choice "

We start at an early age to pick our friends at play, never really giving it much thought as we go on our way.
It seem to not matter much for it's okay in... our book, for we're the same age group and we know what it took.
To stand by each other's side and be there daily in pride, is what we experience every day as we walk along in stride.

Now the time has come that we wise up..... before it takes a toll, for now we see the importance of life, as it is on a roll.
It's dear to be friendly and bond in peace and love, as long as we consider it to be... "A Grown-up Choice" coming from above.
When we look up and get help we fare better in our trend, and now we realize "A Grown-up Choice"... is from within.

" Silent "

Words are gracefully thought of as eyes... behold the sky. Speaking melody in the.... heart, as angels sing in ears of people in tune to God.
Freshly the day bursts upon the morning softly as the birds feel a sprinkle of rain. They flutter their wings and soar toward the sky in delight of home.

* *

" Caught In The Storm "

You started out in life going dearly on your way,
You experience many things that came but no to stay.
You braced yourself with wisdom and understanding too,
You did mostly what your dear parents taught you to do.
You grew up and ventured out into the world but not alone,
You looked around and found that...... family and friends had not gone.
You found that they would stand by your side in a many thing,
You learned early that encouragement gave you a song to sing.
You now are happy and freedom is in a place of welcomed relief,
You know of these things because when "Caught In The Storm" you held on to... your belief.

" It's Not That Bad Right Now "

You know in life we often think that things are really bad,
But nearly three years from now we... say it's not the toughest time I've had.
Now if it's not that bad further down the road...why do we carry the load?

* *

" We Must Sacrifice "

In order to get a gain as we venture
through trials, we will encounter...
many friends that give a lot of smiles.
Daily we experience the workweek or
are retired and all set,
Or we haven't experienced the work
scene being we're too young as yet.
We reach to goals and compare them
sometimes with a friend,
Afterwards we reach to wisdom and
start a dream to defend.
We can't get there overnight for we
will experience just a few delays, yet
we press for it never really stays.
Now we mostly know how we get to
finish what we start,
"We Must Sacrifice" our time and...
most nearly have it in our heart.

" Start In A Corner "

I don't know if you've heard this to
be a real fact, but I was told when I
was young to find a corner before I
act. I was told in order to clean a
room or pack for a move, I needed
to "Start In A Corner" and I did it
to prove. That I was listening to all
they had to say, and I use the same
idea even still on today.

* *

" When You Go Online "

There's a lot of computer whiz out there
and are very happy too,
For they are in tune to e-mails as they
promptly send them through.

After going to work and being on the
computer most of the day,
They come home sometimes tired but...
after dinner they're on their way.

Concerned for their friends and the mail
that's now at hand,
They get a second wind to answer e-mails
as if it's a dear demand.

It fares better for them to clear the junk
mail as sent their way,
They press the delete button and it disap-
pears for they want it not to stay.

After work sometimes it's relaxing to be
an encouragement after you dine,
For your buddies dearly search for your
kindness "When You Go Online."

" Inspiration "

Touching God without calling His name,
after all who's up in the sky? We say don't
let life pass you by, yet it means the same.

* *

" Taking In The View "

**Shopping may not take that long if you
press on your way,
Yet people need encouragement as you
venture every day.
You may be at the grocery store and
continue to converse in the line,
It will make you and them feel better,
as you leave there feeling fine.**

**You've reached out to someone with a
smile or a few words,
You've enhanced their life and they will
remember what they heard.
Then as you walk outside and go on to
another store of your choice,
There's always someone there that would
love to hear your voice.**

**Now other people look at you without....
saying a word, yet they smile,
For they were not directly in the conver-
sation that they heard for a while.
People have a way of picking up bits and
pieces of conversation as they go,
Some just stand there "Taking In The
View" and silently being in the know.
Oh, they absorb the things you've said,
you see it on their face,
As they leave now refreshed, with more
encouragement to run the race.**

* *

" How To Find A Friend "

**Do you look for years or months to be
in the presence of a caring soul,
Or do you just behave in a manner that
you were taught of old.**

**It's apparent that people have a real joy
that they would like to share,
When they reach out to you and find that
you are positioned there.**

**The morning hours are beautiful, with...
lunchtime set for a test,
For it takes you to a grand evening if you
perform your best.**

**Now the time has come that we must.....
search out to people for a lift,
All the time knowing that it's not a tough
time, it's really a gift.**

**Be good to yourself and every day look...
within your heart,
For that's how we make it through life
we do our part.**

**It's not hard to be kind and show love to
all helping them to win,
And to show yourself kind and friendly
is... "How To Find A Friend."**

* *

" Don't Try So Hard "

**Things will work out in your life keep
the faith and promises too,
For God has much power, grace and
mercy to get you through.**

**Relax when you can and don't be so
concerned about reaching your goal,
For what God has for you, your eyes
and hands will behold.**

**There's no need to fret for life may just
want to pass you by,
If you don't give all your situations to
God and look toward the sky.**

**You may want to press every day, and
it will suffice your point of view,
Yet you won't be the one that will dearly
get you through.**

**Without God, we may as well hang up the
towel so to speak,
For the Word of God tells us to speak as...
strong, when we're weak.**

**Now God knows your heart, and the mes-
sage of your prayers that you pray,
So all you need to do is have hope in the
Lord, and go diligently on your way.**

Choosing and selecting friends is not the issue here, for when we show ourselves friendly it ... leads the way to a lifetime friendship.

Economic wearing away separate and move farther.... our friendship and friends. We must overlook the economic differences and strive to have a wholesome friendship, fellowship, and... a peaceful state of mind...find happiness within.

As we revisit friends and journey home we have what one calls victory over hurdles in our lives. For once, and again we have done what is rewarding and feel good about ourselves.

Revisiting friends makes one feel better about life and our outlook on life. If at this time you... can not revisit friends be sure and be a friend to yourself. The word "re" is the great comeback. To do again, holds fairly well in this troubled world, when speaking of friendship and happy times.

What one talks about during sessions of uplifting conversation will have an enduring outlook on the future. Just to think oneself friendly does not heighten friendship...but to be friendly will bring about an action of wit.

Being oneself, advancing in a troubled world ...as writers of poetry, and readers of the same, continue to read "*The Ring Of Friends: Forever*" in all essence of understanding.

Serene as the day and night, with quietness in your heart ...follow your dreams. Peaceful as the midnight hours, with concerns on your mind.... look to God, for He knows all.

Pressing onward through the early morning hours, you realize that you've passed over into another grandeur of victory over your tests ... and trials.

No matter how life seems to be overbearing and unfair hold to God, your integrity and.... family and friends. Here I consider family as friends...and vice versa.

Let your neighbor, coworker, and your family open to you a world as never before as you venture on to read and continue your journey.

Many people enjoy poetry of all types and on views of interest, yet many want simplicity and in general every day life poetry.

As you read along you will find poems to .... your liking and can be read at your leisure. As an adjustment in life read on, and you will be amazed at the words of inspiration and heartfelt freedom it sends to its readers.

In your leisure time, you may venture to a ... world of ease and powerful thinking, only to be left with a... higher state of esteem.

Being that you have at least picked up this... book, you will hopefully come out ahead with uplifted spirits, settled hearts, minds, obtained only but touching the power of God through... His people, and His Word.

Christians, laypersons, adults and children... will all advance with at least higher hopes in... every day life...by reading good quality poetry.

People nowadays, desire more out of life, that will have an inspirational bearing on their life.

* *

" What You Are To Me "

**You are the sunshine upon the window pane,
You are the radiance that do help me to gain.**

**You are the angel I search for in my dream,
You are the fulfillment of friendship it seems.**

**You are the blessing that others call chance,
You are the spirit of freshness in a rain dance.**

**You are there when I need your dear support,
You are the essence of kindness that is sought.**

**You are the lunchtime release to free my mind,
You are a dear friend and you are really kind.**

**You go out your way to say kind things in love,
You go farther to meet me as kindness of a dove.**

**You have the love that is from God and so free,
You have the silence in your presence with me.**

**You sometimes say much and at times not a lot,
You are pressed upon by situations you've got.**

**You are a comfort in the midnight hours too,
You are the bond that keeps me going through.**

**You are a portion that life offers of God above,
"What You Are To Me," you show by your love.**

* *

" The Midnight Hours "

It's a test to press pass the time at the top
of the clock,
When things come on heavy and seem as
firm as a rock.

It's when mostly everyone else is resting
and is fast asleep,
It's now a time that you solemnly being
alone do reap.

Yet you are not all by yourself you have
the Lord for a friend,
You also have one naturally and then the
Lord spiritually to the end.

It's mostly a trial and a time..... for your
thoughts to defend,
Defend them from negatives and you will
definitely win.

You know that the morning light will soon
give you more power to stand,
So keep the faith when......"The Midnight
Hours" are passing through the land.

It gets rough on some and then it's easier
for them to go on their way,
For they have come through "The Midnight
Hours"... that didn't really stay.

* *

" The City Life "

To take the train or a trolley sends a
message of communication,
When it is set to be pertinent in our
wonderful segment of a nation.

We can tell you very well if a stranger
from elsewhere walks in,
For they have a look and a character
they need to defend.

Now we work, we play, and the lights
here never really go out,
We're satisfied in our location without
a shadow of a doubt.

Sometimes we sit at the kitchen table or
in the dining area to converse,
Mostly because we like to entertain and
we'd like to prepare food first.

We can sit for hours on end and watch
the travelers pass,
In a hurried state to reach home...after
getting off from work at last.

We will welcome you through our town
for it is yours too,
And you then will learn "The City Life"
...and what we daily do.

* *

" The Country Life "

We are not as hurried as we go on our
way to pay our dues,
Sometimes we are lost in the shuffle and
people don't have any clues.

They don't have a clue how we entertain
in this style of living,
Neither do they realize that it's all in the
heart of giving.

We give of our time, our life... we share
the market's goal,
We want the same thing and we try what
we've been told.

It's great to be in this place that we have
chosen to be in,
It's a peaceful harmony of birds and the
many marvelous friends.

The gardens are grand...if you decide to
plant one to see it grow,
A wholesomeness of food from the earth
so that "The Country Life" you'd know.

It's growing up fast and trees now seem to
disappear off the land,
But as the process takes its place we yet...
make "The Country Life"...stand.

* *

“ Priorities ”

**We have “Priorities” and we try to sort
them out at our best,
Time presses on us as more things on…
the list will test.**

**They will test our nature and goodwill
to press on,
Sometimes they’re here so fast then so
quickly gone.**

**Who’s to really say when “ Priorities ”
are on the list as high,
When we push to get it all done as time
seems to be nigh.**

**Oh well, do the most important they…
say or make the solemn call,
That would enhance your work and
make you feel so tall.**

**So set out to do it first, and secondly
there’s something else for you to do,
All because the one thing before it…
will want its priority too.**

**You must get your rest so you sort out
your errands and go,
Now who really is wise would let their
“Priorities”...show.**

* *

" Whilst At Home "

I feel the sense of security as I awaken
from a restful sleep today,
I had a many concern but I removed it
before bedtime so it could not stay.
I went through the day encouraged for
it means a lot at the end,
I was not bogged down with trials for
I tossed them to the wind.
I had an easy day for a friend I knew
dropped by to say hello,
I was really glad to converse but then
they really had to go.

I'm really thankful that I was remem-
bered from years back,
I remember now when I had to move
and they came over to help me pack.
I'll get to see them again, for I know
how I can reach them once more,
I can build a friendly foundation again
as in school, we did adore.

I feel relieved, and I'm on my way from
work, now to pack my things to depart,
I will have a pleasant night for "Whilst
At Home" I searched my heart.
I searched my heart to be friendly, greet-
ing patrons and friends with smiles,
I prayed to God "Whilst At Home" and
now it has taken me through my trials.

* *

" Winter Soup "

Oh, the essence of the season with friends getting together,
Even if it's a press they try to meet in any kind of weather.

Oh, to go to the store and shop galore for many fun things,
When the season brings in the pleasant... times and familiar rings.

Let the treetops be decked with an array of snow frosted tops,
For the essence of the season with family, and friends never stops.

Gather at home, or for a change go over and visit a friend,
As they welcome you with warmth, as you are asked to come in.

Then to sit and talk about the good times that you've had,
Cheering each other letting them know things aren't that bad.

The season will be cozy, caring, breezy and free...it all is well,
For you'll have "Winter Soup" right there where you dwell.

* *

" Soup With Friends "

Of all the things we could think of for the
season and winter glee,
We would like to shop and especially make
an effort to trim a tree.

Now that it is over with so soon, and we have
a little time to spare,
We would like to experience a wonderful...
heartfelt care.

So we make a phone call, or we send an...
e-mail just to see,
If either one of us will be busy, or will be
immediately free.

For there's something cooking and it's...
savory with spice,
Just to be together, like family and to be
really very nice.

The warmth of the feeling just to visit and
to stay awhile,
Whilst we share photo albums and we let
go of a smile.

There's nothing like being in the presence
of caring people and feeling free,
For having "Soup With Friends" is a real
blessing to you and me.

* *

" Soup With Givens "

Let's get out the bowls, bring on the spoons,
For we will be conversing, and uplifted soon.
Times has come, we need a lift to get through,
Be reassured as the poetry reading bless you.

Oh, the sounds of the words in the air as free,
The nice aroma of soup is passed along to me.
I pass it on to my friend that's seated nearby,
We settle into peace and harmony that is nigh.

Just to warm also the heart, of poet to friend,
We reminisce, we express where we've been.
You're welcomed in this place, this wonderful
land, I thought to place warmth in your heart
and "Soup With Givens" in your hand.

What better way to enjoy your soup than with
a good poem, people often daily read poetry...
and that's the norm.
Having soup is of a fine quality, it gives you...
time to really bond,
Have "Soup With Givens" and daily make ...
your poetic heart more fond.

Have many happy days, and when you have
reached your goal to succeed,
It would be a great idea to have a bowl of ...
"Soup With Givens"..... and poetry to read.

* *

" I Remember When "

Conversation is pleasant and going very
well, feelings are there, we can really tell.

We have reached out to others to express
our hope, being together we can now cope.

We do need each other, we knew years ago,
We were in school and into the college flow.

Time has passed we still can see the need,
To be a family with friends as we succeed.

Some have moved on, took another road,
Some stayed together to yet carry the load.

Mocking bird tweets in the tree of its choice,
It expresses that it's aware it still has a voice.

We talk to each other every now and then,
At times we both say "I Remember When."

" Wintry Day "

Oh, to warm by the compassion of a lovely
heart is it a dream, or a reality that is ....
found in only a few,
When close friends reach to the neighbors
for help, let it be in you.
Be it grand to compose a sonnet and let it go
away, it'd be like a kite on a "Wintry Day."

* *

" Church "

A place of worship for grown-ups and children too,
You needed a plan for worship and God has given it to you.

From times of old you were told of God's Divine Word,
And you've learned to live from all that... you've heard.

So find one and then go to a "Church" of your own choice,
And then you can worship the Lord there and lift up your voice.

" Hopeful Days "

The time we're living in calls for a lot of hope, people are in need of assistance to help them cope.

Yet if they'd go to the Lord and ask Him for help, they will have prayers answered and also be kept.

So ever look to God for encouragement, your needs and care, for He from days of old have always met us there.

* *

" Spiritual Thoughts "

Just riding along today, humming a
song, meditating that God is strong.
He will take you through life and care
for you each day, all you need to do is
live for Him, and believe when you pray.

You're not alone, in this big world by...
yourself we hear, and the Word of God
stands sure, when evil thoughts are near.
Diligently look to God, and rest in His
love, get all you need in life from the ...
Blessed God above.

" Dealing With Life"

Years ago I was told to cope with a
situation, for I was not the only one,
but it even sweeps the nation.
That gave me hope to really know...
God would be with me wherever I
would go.
And all in all, as a pleasant surprise,
the whole enlightenment opened up
my eyes.
So in order for us all to daily cope,
we must look to God and His Word...
and live in hope.
So "Dealing With Life" will be easy ...
then, as we allow the Lord to within
our hearts...come in.

* *

" A Friend "

One who cares, really cares. It matters not the day or the hour, they will be by your side with power.
No adjustment needed for "A Friend," as you blossom without and within.

" Friends "

They come to you everyday, did you see them on your way. You passed them on yesterday, the one that had something they wanted to say.
Do you remember the one I mean, when they waved when you were seen. The one that called with a love note, the one that sent the letter they wrote.
The one that helped to make ends meet, they are "Friends" and are really neat.

" Friendly "

Blessing people touching their lives in words, with the real action of your deeds. Will rightly express a lovely gesture….. planting the friendship seeds. You being you to help us along, being "Friendly" …remaining strong.

* *

" A Need "

Pressing past thoughts of others. God keeps the notes. Within my heart, I do endeavor to make a start.
Placid feelings greatly coming from my thoughts. I now have spoken it into.... existence and it is fulfilled in my heart.

" A Want "

A lot, a little just to even it out. Over-filled, yet to restore, mostly at one time. Neighbors check out its lot, and department store's galore. It presses upon me today, as I receive it fully.

" A Wish "

A blow into the wind, yet captured upon the shore. It's thought upon, it's reached yet, will it show upon the morn.
A greatness of friendship to an outgoing smile. May it reach its goal, and my eyes behold its happiness as it's passed on to others along the way.

"A Fad "

Can you start one all by yourself, or do you need a friend, for if you wanted to it would be everyone's choice in the end.

* *

" Alone "

You are you. Peaceful thoughts now run through your mind. Yet you have a friend within yourself.

Look into your heart and warm in the.... "love" of your heart. Cares will then release themselves.....and a phone call may just show up from a friend.

" Lonely "

Do we always have a need for people to be around. Memories are truly refreshing to a distant view. When we look into the mirror of hope we find a peace in our heart.

Integrity is holding steadily in our minds... as we drift off into a restful sleep. Most... things are better by morning as we awaken with a victorious smile.

" Free "

To be, to glance, to advance to a level of helpful resolve. Like the birds of flight... drifting wholesomely on its way.

The day is grand, love is in your heart, the world is at your feet, and you bless the very presence of friends with your goodness.

* *

" As One "

It seems like the whole world is at ease.
To press toward your goals in peaceful
ways with others.
Them reaching out to your hand, you
knowing it's real to be a part of it all.
Things work out and it's like family...
and friends everywhere you go.

" Together "

A lot of people, putting in their hands
to make a feasible advancement. It's not
only nice, it's a form of a miracle bestow-
ed from above.
Nothing will really stop the progress of
these people and hindrance must leave
its post.
Pressed upon with diligence, negatives
takes its flight. It's a proven fact that...
mountains do move.

" A Group "

To gather in another city or in this town
matters not. To team in colors of victory
is all the better.
To be set apart in wholesome avenues of
worth. To show the world it can be done.
Yes, to be led, to be followed for we've
won. Many times over everyday we're...
seen in each other as we pass by.

* *

" No Time To Read "

Oftentimes you tell me that you're busy
and schedule is full,
You just can't get out a book and the...
load's tough to pull.
Some people are writers and some just
love to open a book,
As they sat down to coffee, or tea and...
took a look.

You say I never do that for I have other
things on my mind,
You remember the times past when time
you would find.
Some people know the joy of reading a...
book all the way through,
For they take the time for themselves...
and for relaxation too.

Now if we weren't so rushed up with all
these cares that we name,
We wouldn't say "No Time To Read,"...
and it would work out the same.

Find time when traveling as a rider, even
when you pay a fare,
Or choose a place of your choice and you
will find encouragement there.

* *

" No Time to Write "

Some are not writers of personal letters
even of short length,
Even though it gives our friends and...
family some strength.

That's okay not to write it day in and...
then day out,
Yet people would love for you to give...
them a shout.

Now it's said time won't really permit
me to do more,
Yet time sometimes slips away from us
right out the door.

Just to jot a few lines to our fellowman
on today,
Will last them until you can get another
on its way.

All of us are not on computers, or an...
e-mail would be the thing,
For sometimes we get an e-mail if the...
mailman doesn't ring.

Give it a chance or get someone else to
write a line,
And the people on the other end will be
feeling just fine.

Enough negativity has already taken over... and must have an override to restore oneself to a reality of good things.

Reading is good for the mind, keeping the right perspective of enriching lives by words of wisdom. Poetry heals minds, and hearts of people that has been hurt, misunderstood, and people not heard either by loneliness or older age and left to oneself.

Poetry also has a way of restoring, and bringing about a good sum of happiness to many... people. Please continue to read and enjoy the many words of comfort found in these poems. Variety has its field day and hearts....get a release on life, and minds......seem to be clearer.

Conclusion in life should take under consideration the length and ...timing of situations. Friends fare better to overlook mere.... small things in life that gender strife.

We all have at times had low tolerance for some state of being. Whether imposing on... one's intelligence to lack of respect for one's character and individuality.

Yet, through it all, things can be so to speak ironed out as we give people a try at life. Give mercy to some, caring to others, all by the.... leadership of God.

The poetry here can be read with an understanding of getting closer to all people in these last and evil days. Whether your status is together or singular, stay free and keep your... mind free and your soul in a state of rejoicing.

Read poetry with a cup of coffee, tea, or... soda pop, but above all enjoy the words and savor it in the light of a better world to come.

God will make all things beautiful in His... own time....as His Word states. Let's keep the ring of friends, and feel....again the kindreds of blessed hope that's...bestowed upon friendships when we share in kindness.

Whether you read silently or out loud may this poetry...leave you with an ease of mind and heart...a breather on life, at last.

God is the only one that really knows our future, rest assured...He is. Yet, He gives an avenue whereby we can survive life's situations, some by writing, reading, singing or... whatever our gifts may be.

We're not left out for God has provided an avenue of escape......we can find it in God's Word, and in inspirational reading. Whether a full course or an appetizer, read until you're satisfied in your individual state of mind and sound being.

In life we need something that will hold our attention and enrich our lives...everything else could possibly be a waste of time and attention. It fares well to enhance our life with good.... wholesome living, helping others along the way with our friendship.

***"The Ring Of Friends: Forever"* .....can only relay a message of friendship upon one's mind and heart. What else can be done is due to individual caring, sharing, and a need to do both.**

* *

" The Best Is Yet To Come "

Ease your mind over life's cares, promises will fall upon listening ears. The promises fulfilled will someday be, and you'll be all the better for it.

Distant hearts wish to be closer, dreams... are pleasant to happy people. Plans are excellent for a marvelous generation as they press into the future.

The family is uplifted, friends are near,... placid conversation is amongst peers. God is good to you and yours and, "The Best Is Yet To Come."

" Just Breezing Through In Life "

It's not good to see a young people that
doesn't have a smile on their face,
After all, look at the grown-ups and all
what they've done to keep the pace.
Isn't it enough that these people are now
young and have a lot of years ahead per se,
And then to look at the examples that the
grown folks have sent their way.
So the next time you see a young person...
frowning, seemingly without a friend,
Go to them or just share a smile so they
know that...life will just now begin.

* *

" Just Get Through It "

Now a pity-party is not the way to go for
it's not like strength,
Of all the things you've been through in
life continue at any length.

It started when you were young and now
times have brought it afar,
All along the way you've struggled and...
you have remained up to par.

It's just the idea of every day life that we
are really concerned about,
Whether it's a tough thing or a thing of
ease it could cause a serious doubt.

We search our minds then seek a family
member, or a friend to assist,
For it's sometimes mind boggling to be
in deep thought with concerns all amidst.

We have to be strong there is no doubt
about it, if we want to really survive,
For we must take things all "one day at
a time," even seconds, to really strive.

It's a way that's not always easy when we
really look at our life as a whole,
Yet, "Just Get Through It" and consider
your faith to be...very bold.

* *

" The Bike Ride "

Oh, how the pedals turn over, strength is in your feet and legs. You're in control of what is the length of your journey. Does it matter, for you have miles to decide.

Perhaps you stop to see a neighbor granted that it's in your heart today. Or, to see a ... grand friend, one that helped you to where you are, or to whom you have become. Does that matter, now that the pedals have brought you here.

Again, your friend was glad to see you, ... with heartfelt feelings of you on yesterday. Now if you were on a stationary bike you would have just dreamed you had fulfilled your plans.

But it's so real for you to feel the breeze upon your brow, and....hear the traffic as it approaches. Whiz, whiz...goes the... spokes as you're now getting a nice stride.

Oh, the essence of the energy that has... brought you thus far. You're now elevated in body, mind and spirit, as the pedals and your feet...take you back home.

* *

" A Walk Through The Land "

You could choose to walk alone or have a friend by your side. It is to the highest hopes, that they are welcomed in.

Now if you want to walk with a friend or a family member be it grand, for you will gather strength being of a positive mind.

The walk could be far or near, yet you'll need a nice conversation along the way. Or, you all could be silent and just think on life and its goodness.

Whatever you decide you will have a wonderful walk...be it first in your heart then you will have patience, and tolerance for flaws. Walk wholesomely, and freely, calling things into memory that's pleasant.

The walk will call for stamina...or catch it in the end as you now arrive near the end of your journey. You may have walked in pairs, be it strength to you and your friend.

Say you have walked alone, you now feel... refreshed, your mind is cleared, and you... will feel better on the morn. Friends will be thankful of your pleasant nature, and your life will be...more richly admired.

* *

" The Fresh Air Of Virginia "

There are cities and towns all around, it's what you choose to do,
From the east to the west, from the north to the south it's all up to you.

Now some prefer the countryside with the trees and lakes of their likes,
Yet some prefer the city life with trolleys, trains, and their personal bikes.

Wherever they go they get the freshness of the breeze that's at hand,
Oh, the wholesome oneness of the wonderful agricultural land.

The morning mostly bring on the breeze... yet the evening takes its turn,
Many now have passed the word of freshness that they want to learn.

To learn of this land Virginia and a people of a kindhearted sort,
As if the sounds of nature to this land has been taught.

Even if you sat on your porch in the city it would be a blessed relief,
Or, in the midst of the country "The Fresh Air Of Virginia" would be your belief.

* *

“ The Breeze Of New Jersey ”

As we sit in the midst of the surroundings
we smile,
For a lot of us have now traveled over a...
many mile.

To get to the East Coast and to take in the
marvelous view,
Some walking, some talking, some holding
hands to get them through.

Now some are in love, and some just travel-
ed to be alone,
Some met friends nearby for dinner to keep
them atone.

The air is so solemn and gives a message of
wonderful glee,
As some patrons sit offshore, where there’s
still a planted tree.

Many people gesture of lovely ways that’s
set in their heart,
As they have nice times amongst friends...
before they depart.

We should build friendship up and keep the
level of it very high,
As we feel “The Breeze Of New Jersey” and
look toward the beautiful sky.

* *

" A Friend Of The Family "

Years have passed since we all came to-
gether for a feast that's annually done,
Phone calls on yesterday brought about
a time of happy laughter as one.

Some of us are not naturally born into
this group of people, so fine,
Yet we still get into the hope of the nice
family, and calling it mine.

People step up to us, and want to really
know about us and our ways,
Whether we've really known each other
for a sum of many years, and days.

It really matters not to us the length of
how long it has been going on,
For when we first met it was like the…
freshness of the morn.

We took to each other as if we'd been
knowing each other all along,
Some of us have grown up around here,
as we've kept each other strong.

So if you'd ask the neighbor of us, so as
to make an introduction,
They'd tell you that we're "A Friend Of
The Family" and under their protection.

* *

" Our Friend "

Call it whatever you would like or say it
is really nice,
Yet I find, that to be friendly calls for a
kind heart, and sacrifice.

For you must then forget yourself, and
your thoughts of concern,
In order to help someone else along the
way to learn.

For in so doing, you will have reached
out to some,
And they will reach out to others as the
dear time come.

You can talk about some of the people
that you mostly meet,
And how they have helped you to stand
firm on your feet.

You can say how they're there upon your
every call,
You could say how they make you feel…
nice and tall.

We must tell you now that it's real grand
for us to hear,
For we have one, … we call "Our Friend"
and they are so dear.

Poetry here, is about every day situations in life, and its scenic views as we journey to and from people that love to be uplifted. Let's start and as many already does…..continue to uplift.

As we are sometimes lost for words, we find comfort and solace in the words of a friend. Come venture along as you read a…collection of poetry suited for the young, the older set… lifting spirits to another level of aspiration.

Take *"The Ring Of Friends: Forever"* along in your travels, and let the words of inspiration fill times of serenity and peace…..adding more power for the journey…..as you journey home after visiting friends.

Come once again to a start of a new day and times in life. Removing doubt, and relaxing in the comfort of best friends, brings the strength level up to another rung on the ladder of hope.

Many subjects are discussed in life but time becomes short as economic values are placed in …our awakened hours. Thereby, we all can but reminisce, be peacefully reminded by words of wisdom and heartfelt visions of the mind.

In life one will pick up a book and read, let… this book be the one after all is said…….for it will enhance your very remarkable thoughts on your journey home from chosen friends, near and far.

We talk about friends here, being that this… book is about feeling good about ourselves and our family and friends. We need compassion… even if done through a counseling spirit…it will not only help us, but also give strength to others.

As we sit, and think it is as if...our forehead is pressing against the universe. Our thoughts reach out to answers as our minds try to get a clear lead way. One of the best thinking positions is the blank wall, look around...a room has four of them.

We wonder how some people could hurt our feelings, or even as we say "go there," but..... many have "went." In life we experience these things but it's better them than you, for the... payday will soon be theirs...so you stay encouraged. If they get in your way...encourage them too, for in years to come or even days they will notice your kindness.

How and why these things happen? Why not? Oh, really?...I'll make it in spite of problems... and troubles, and you will too. Providing you... fight with integrity, backbone, and spunk. Get to the bottom of things, come to grips, and then go on...with "your life."

Things could always be worse in our lives. In the mind there's a press for answers and sometimes it's found in our hearts. Encourage people, have the love for people regardless of the depth of pain. Oh, a breath of relief, a sigh, a relaxation process for us all, as we realize our limitations. We're destined to make it through by.... faith, hope, love, and by the mercy and grace of Almighty God.

Never knowing what's on a person's mind.... should keep ours in check. How they have come through some era in their life...is a mindful task. Spare grief, pain,...help someone along the way.

* *

" A Trip For Two "

Tis, to leave is to return, wishing for the time to continue on for more,
Oh, to see the oceans and the ships come in from a distant shore.

And to be enhanced by the beautiful rays of the morning sunlight,
Causes our days to be wholesome, with a great delight.

Something we've planned, and it has ran its course of days,
And now is performed before our eyes as we see "live plays."

How wonderful this is, together with each other and free,
That cast a brightness of blue skies and ... white clouds to see.

To travel together we reminisce of early times when we met,
When times were not as tough, and trials were not set.

To do a thing together fares better for us both as one,
As we keep the friendship going..."A Trip For Two" is done.

* *

" A Lovely Trip "

We leave at an early time for we want to
get a good start,
We gather all our things, also something
close to our heart.

It's good to take along a remembrance...
from home to go along,
If things didn't go as planned it would...
keep us strong.

Take along an inspiration, or two to take
up the space,
When you would stand in line and need
mercy and grace.

We relax, relate, release the pressures...
that do appear,
Some things in life can be handled if we
keep them near.

So that they get nipped in the bud, and
cause no other concern,
As it was told of our parents, and it was
something to learn.

We now have "A Lovely Trip" for we....
had advice before we did start,
For we whispered...a prayer to the Lord,
and He answered us in our heart.

* *

" A Family Gathering "

**All of family who choose to come in, may enter now therein,
We thought to receive you gently, also as a comfort and friend.**

**We've planned this for sometime, and am now really glad,
That we now realize how many of family and friends we had.**

**It's so nice to be associated with others... and be called family and friend,
When the introduction is brought about it's glorious to reverse the trend.**

**The food galore is heartily arrayed for us all to dine,
We're pleasantly reminiscing, and we're feeling just fine.**

**We show kindness for our individuality... having respect, dignity and love,
We are wholesomely enthused, sharing it greatly as given from above.**

**It's "A Family Gathering" as the sum of the crowd turn out,
As we enjoy ourselves to the fullest, and without any doubt.**

* *

" A Job Luncheon "

Let's just make the best of the dear time
at hand,
Being relaxed now as we converse, share
and understand.

It's wholesome to get together and enjoy
the time spent,
For whilst we're at work, it's like the.....
time just went.

Now you don't really have to try to keep
the score,
As the dishes are passed around and as...
coworkers ask for more.

It leads into the evening hours...we think
on giving the job our best,
Giving coworkers the option now of pure
relaxation, and rest.

Depending on the occasion, we think it to
be just great,
To have "A Job Luncheon" planned again
we can hardly wait.

It gives us time to get a release, to bond...
and be free,
To also fill our heart's desire, and then we
leave..."at three."

* *

" When We Met "

Friendship is so wonderful and powerful to be in,
We did not know that we would eventually meet a friend.

The school days fade away, and our age now upon us gain,
As our hearts are close together and love in it remain.

We looked to each other at first, but not as a friend,
But realized later, that to find one, we had to begin.

We moved on to friendship as we stood … and spoke in the class,
We sang of our "Alma Mater," a song for us all at last.

Now we are friends and enjoy the… goodness that it brings,
When concerned, we always call, or surely the doorbell rings.

Just to say we care, and are there for each other's needs,
We're glad that "When We Met,"…we've done our good deeds.

* *

“ You ”

We do get rest and play, after all life is
at times really fun,
We tell our friends of our many wonder-
ful days in the sun.

We do a lot of things that could include
“one” or “two,”
Yet sometimes “we”... will be able to in-
clude also a few.

We are mostly satisfied with the many...
friends of our choice,
It’s not always in a long conversation....
but in a compassionate voice.

And what about yourself, when you look,
yet can’t find a friend,
Remember the same heart is there, for...
“You” to look within.

“ Give Yourself Some Credit ”

Now we’re not saying you always need a
pat on the back to make it, even if your
friends weren’t around you’d ride off in-
to the sunset and take it.
Yet, it will dearly mean a lot when it is...
coming from a friend,
But even at that, you must upon God....
and you...depend.

* *

" For The Life Of Us "

What rendition, what an adventure, when
we've reached to a friend,
For life has its own song, of great grandeur
in the end.

What a patriotic duty of our homeland...
where we live,
For life has its own essence, of a personal
thing that we give.

What glory and honour that we give to ...
Our Master up above,
For life has its own time, to embrace and...
give us love.

What an amazement of our heroes as they
firmly stand,
For life has its own enactment, of your own
place in this land.

What a solemn choice of people as we gath-
er together as one,
For life has its own destiny, let it be for all
the best things done.

" Ever Learning, Ever Changing"

Everything is not for everybody, every day is not the same. Some can see, yet many, yet look. Yet, keep integrity, yet, moving in life.

* *

" A Wonderful Life "

**To be a child blessed in a land of free-
dom as you were reared, being fed the
Word of God for your parents feared.**

**The fear was not of a sudden thing but
to the Lord in reverenced respect, then
you'd follow Him in love and connect.**

**To be found as a child in your eyes and
in your heart just as well, is a purity of a
child that at a glance the world can tell.**

**You will have then a sense of compassion
on your fellowman every day, for you'll
be in tune to what your heart has to say.**

**Your friends will be plentiful with a re-
hearsal of your dreams, when you looked
beyond people's faults with love it seems.**

**Things will be a blessing you're at ease...
and tears will be at a lost, for you'll find
friends come to you truly without a cost.**

**In your beautiful hometown to another...
town on the coast, you search out to see...
"A Wonderful Life" you wanted the most.**

* *

" Story Of Life "

Do you have a "Story Of Life" to help others along the way,
Hold it not in for people need to hear it on every day.

How you reared your children, with... the help of God and His love,
With the firmness of your hand, yet... the loving heart of a dove.

Blessing people along the way not only family and friends,
For the stranger that you met on yesterday may be a friend before it ends.

Keep yourself available, help others also without a frown,
For you've been over that road and you have been around.

The "Story Of Life" as you tell it...being overheard by a stranger at the store,
Will save a life from misery and they may seek God all the more.

"The World Waits "

Someone has to do it, be it not you? The first time, it didn't work, try it again too.
The spirit of love, and compassion in you.

* *

" Story Of Victory "

You tell a "Story Of Victory" as you call
up a friend to say hello,
They in turn lift you up too and now you
are happy as you go.

If you have a "Story Of Victory" your....
family and friends need to know,
For they can witness it with their life and
have progress as they grow.

Let's spread out the cheer of triumphs for
we have been through it,
Help them please and show them...the wis-
dom of how to do it.

It doesn't take a strong person to have .....
power, only endure as God has said,
And you will be an example, positively of
people you will be read.

They will look at your life and say my, my,
they are really blessed in their deed,
So tell your "Story Of Victory" and help...
someone else to succeed.

"The People's Needs "

Someone is going to survive, let it be also
by your hand, calling into remembrance
how you prayed...then made your stand.

* *

" Words To A Child "

**When you express anything to a child be
sincere and show love every day,
For these little ones will then hold it in....
their hearts and minds to stay.**

**If they don't get guidance to erase the ....
damage that could be long,
It will become a part of them and it will ...
follow them as strong.**

**Most people know how to talk to a child ...
for we were one ourselves,
And our parents taught us well, it wasn't
to be put back on the shelves.**

**These dear people need your help in the
community, one at a time will do,
For if it's to become a reality of lovely ...
ways, it must first come from you.**

**So watch the "Words To A Child" for it...
will leave a mark that's not easy to forget,
For a better choice of words will help them
to be better, and then good things will set.**

" Child "

Mild mannered bunch of energy, with all questions set up front. At times, they are to be listened to...cooperating with their wish.

* *

" Words To An Adult "

Now some adults can't take everything...
that you blurt out on your way,
Therefore take hold of your "Words To
An Adult"...that you do say.

Some will blot it from their minds for they
know the shoe doesn't fit,
But some will take it to heart and it will ...
then dull their wit.

Go on with your life, even though trials...
touch your very heart,
For God never changes and remember ...
He's the very same from the start.

Let your choice of words not have partial-
ity and show love to your fellowman,
Let your choice of "Words To An Adult"
be words that help them stand.

You don't want a stumbling block in your
way, by people's words as they converse,
So have a good choice of words in your...
heart, before your mind rehearse.

" Adult "

Way, way grown with some childlike ges-
tures. Call it young at heart, we wait our
turn....only thing it's the grown-up child.

* *

" Words To A Teenager "

Now this is a subject that we pass over
every day as small,
Yet if it's not addressed or nipped…in
the bud it will become tall.

So the "Words To A Teenager" should
be choice and taught by your example,
For after your "Words To A Teenager"
they will search for your sample.

How you keep your tone of voice very
soft, showing love to teenagers today,
Will really benefit them, and keep it
in their young minds to stay.

They're a nice group of people, but do
hurt their feelings, please be nice,
They offer to you a smile, that you …..
should send to them, more than twice.

They go through times of trials, times
with a mixture in their mind,
As they look to a mentor, that makes
them feel free, and is kind.

" Teenager "

Wholesomely ecstatic, flowing through
times thus far. Their questions have now
been asked, self-answered by, "I know."

* *

" Words To A Student "

Whether it's before kindergarten or in
the first grade of school,
Let your sound choice of "Words To A
Student" be of the golden rule.

Young minds at work in the educational
field could use your guide,
Pump them up to the levels that they too
will take life in stride.

When they're in grade school, help them
to reach the level of highness,
They will appreciate your efforts and one
day will to you confess.

That the words you said to them helped
them to embrace the storm,
And if they never tell you of the victory
it will be of no harm.

For your "Words To A Student" were...
expressed by you in love as embraced,
And one day someone helped you along
the way through trials you have faced.

" Student "

Gathering education by means of a past
scholar, that has reached their goals, and
returned to society, the lessons learned.

* *

" Words To An Enemy "

The choice of words are important yet
may be few,
For the enemy is one that will help you
to get through.

They are there for a reason and say ....
kind things to them today,
Brush yourself off, get help from God
and dearly go on your way.

Let your "Words To An Enemy" show
love for God requires it of you,
In order to get to Heaven it is something
we all must do.

They might thank you one day and say...
you're the nicest person they've met,
It will be grand for them, and for you ....
your Christian life is set.

The nice "Words To An Enemy" will then
show them that you still care,
And you can wish them Heaven's best, or
say, "Just be there."

" Enemy "

The ones that God uses to His Glory, by...
turning curses into blessings, negatives....
into positives. God gives power over them.

* *

" Words To A Friend "

Hold the hand of a friend, for they will
feel like family it's true,
We are given this blessing of friends....
and it's dearly set for you.

When expressing "Words To A Friend"
keep their feeling guarded with love,
For they're people too, and also show
the kindness as of a dove.

Show them your peaceful ways, and let
your words to them enhance,
The goodness that God has shown to...
you, giving them a chance.

A chance to fulfill their life, with just a
little help from you will do,
As your "Words To A Friend" build up
their zeal, sending love back to you.

It's easy to be nice to a friend, for they
were a stranger only for a while,
"Words To A Friend" will help them, to
help others to reconcile.

" Friend "

Feeling alike, yet maybe apart. Lovely,
longsuffering personality, of hopes are
being desired, by one such as them.

* *

" Fiction "

Now to tell a story of "Fiction" is a way
to express a point,
Yet don't hand things out to people ....
giving them everything they want.

For the mind should be pure and, not ...
put hurt into the process,
And the heart should be real and true....
thereby, you can confess.

That parables are used to bring things
on a level for us to all learn,
Yet keep the morals in the story and the
pay that we will earn.

If we reap then what we sow, for that is
what we will do,
We will learn from such an example of
"Fiction" and bring our life anew.

" Era Of The Brouth On The Brow "

Oh, how the brouth breaketh on the brow
Sending a chase to the inner leaves
Smiling upon faces golden in hue
Once more then we say, it's finished
Breaking the brouth bows on the morning
When the eagles flitters solemnly on
Wholesomely ecstatic pressing forth now
Breaketh the brouth calling it an era.

* *

" Truth "

It's Ultimate and Divine, no ifs, ands,
or buts to see,
For "It," "Truth" stands by itself, and
not need you or me.

When we tell it like it is, and call a tree
a tree, by its name,
We will all live a better life, and treat...
all people the same.

When a person is wrong whether family,
friend or foe today,
It doesn't erase the fact that they were...
wrong in this way.

Yet we can support them and being an...
example sent from God to help,
By so doing, a dear soul knows of the....
"Truth" to be dearly kept.

" Oh God, Please Have Mercy "

Now, some of these people are walking
around here, trying to breeze by,
Not always mentioning your Name, Dear
Lord, unless a pain causes them to cry.
Then they call out your Name saying,....
"Oh God, Please Have Mercy"on dear me,
As other people look around to observe,
that it came home to them, finally.

Speaking of "helping someone, along the way," it's a regular saying but.....when you mix encouragement, into it, you're on your way to lifetime's rewards...to yourself, and others. It'll be great for them, and yourself.

Now, the mind relaxes, from the quest of knowing, all because it has reached its goal. Relax and relate, and you will release a .... many pressures...in life. Only think with ... your head up, not down. Thinking with a... downward position of the head, has a mild tendency to bring one's spirit low. Okay, ... that's the reason a person says..."keep your chin up," they mean well by this saying.

Cruising the mind with hope, helps you to reach out to others...alongside helping oneself. Be ever mindful, that what goes around comes around. On the merry-go-round, the same horse you got on, at the entrance, will be the horse you get off, at your destination.

What will it hurt to be nice to people?...... Yes, they may just take your loyal kindness for granted, but they might just learn from... your example...we need to, "go there."

Some of us try so hard in life, it reminds... me of the "touch lamp," the more you touch it, it gets brighter, then eventually goes out. But try, not trying so hard, let life flow, as... the water brook, unclogging issues of life.

Some people, will put a strain on your life, let it be a lesson to you....learn it in levels of harmony and peace. Your destiny, will ever be at hand, so ....live life to its fullest state.

You can not alter the changes in life by your constant, disgruntled moods, but ... by intense prayer and praise to God.

I've thought on many subjects, views,... for this book, and have found an easy format. Poetry should be read for hours in... ease and I thought to do so......by reading them firsthand, in a left to right style, it's easier on the eyes than centered work.

Some poems are extended, yet simple to read, at times life is extended and simple. I thought it to be, with all good intentions, a blessing as you read, at your own speed of reading, and at whatever intervals in your spare time...it's your life...enjoy it.

I've been told by some, that they've been very attentive to reading this poetry, and was reluctant to put the book down,...yet, to keep the family happy, they put it down long enough, to prepare dinner...amazing.

This book will perhaps not be read all in one sitting, as the other two poetry books, being that it has more volume, and is to be in lovely graceful ways an attention holder.

Reading in a relaxed state, our eyes can follow along in ease, as we curl up in the nook with this book for it's okay....it stays soft from the front to the back of this book. You can relax, for it's smooth, and you will not have to brace for what's coming in the next verse, it makes for a wonderful mood. Let's continue this journey of peaceful and wisdom based poetry, let's be happy in life.

* *

" I Will Write "

**I will write the words that come to me,
Even if they do not always come to be.**

**I will write the words that touch my life,
It may just add to someone some spice.**

**I will write as feelings move on their way,
As I listen to what people have to say.**

**I will write whilst I'm very young at heart,
Encouraging others as from the very start.**

**I will write through the freedom of words,
As I seek distant horizons as I have heard.**

**I will write reaching horizons in my mind,
I will encourage the many people that I find.**

**I will be very inspired every day and night,
My blessings are in the power of my might.**

**The might of my pen as it now glides as free,
And as it stir up the marvelous poetry in me.**

**The Lord gives me what I need for the might,
For when young I found poetry in my sight.**

**I will publish a book with my words within,
If my very wholesome dreams I do defend.**

* *

" A Woman's Decree "

I will vary my strength, to survive the days,
I will depend on God, and friends who stays.
I will be encouraged to stay focused and free,
I will be a woman fully, that in my heart is me.
I will be in strong resolve, leading women on,
I will work quilting words that in me are born.
I will be love that's planted in everyday's rose,
I'll be what "A Woman's Decree" is I suppose.

" A Right Now Poem "

We might as well converse, things could
always be worse.
We might as well cheer each other up, for
God has love for our cups.
Don't put off giving up some daily cheer,
don't let it be like I'm the only one here.
I need encouragement as well as you, so be
kind, and send me some cheer too.

" Only By God "

When we get the *I wills*, state them very clear,
If not for the Lord, dreams could not appear.
When we get the *I dos*, state it proudly as nice,
If God didn't give us grace, we'd think twice.
When we get the *I ams*, state them as a pause,
If God don't give mercy, we'd have no cause.
When we get the *I cans*, state them as humble,
If God don't broaden our scope, we'd stumble.

* *

" Bedroom Prayer "

**Bless us, of this room, with peace and love,
Given of, Our Heavenly Father, God above.
Bless our thoughts, and give us ease of rest,
Knowing that, God knows what's really best.
Clear our minds, giving us thoughts so pure,
Raising our great level of strength to endure.**

" Bathroom Prayer "

**Bless this room, and us with a peaceful resolve,
For this is the room, used for things we solve.
It's sometimes a private room, we find of glee,
When we are at rest, and... finally feeling free.**

" Kitchen Prayer "

**Bless this room and us, with warmth of heart,
Helping us all to daily chip in, and do our part.
We're here, and will make the best of our days,
Cooking with love, now that will show, it pays.**

" Living Room Prayer "

**Bless this room, and us, as we're here to smile,
All the time we get to be in here, a great while.
A place that we need a lot of blessings to be in.
We have our family, and friend's minds to win.
For we must keep watch, on the television set,
All is not wholesome, and still need prayer yet.**

* *

" All Through The House Prayer "

Blessings seem to now, fall from the air,
Especially when the Lord meet you there.

Walk through blessing the house is gain,
After the blessed prayer all hope remains.

Talking to the Lord, from room to room,
Whether vacuuming or using the broom,

This is something that we all expect to do,
Living alone, or whether more than two.

To bless the rooms, as you dearly pass by,
Or to stop by and stay a while, you do try.

Be it in company, or whether alone today,
Prayer takes place, as you're on your way.

No need to pick out different words to use,
It accomplishes the same results you choose.

You say a host of words as the night arrive,
It matters not of words, but how you strive.

Striving to be whole, with freedom's light,
Prayer, a way to happiness it's of your right.

Sunlight presses upon the window somehow,
As you do,"All Through The House Prayer."

* *

" Months "

(Part I)

January **is the month of a winter breeze that soothes our minds of thoughts, of concerns. We are happy.**

February **is the month of solemn sounds of softness, words of warmth. Greetings are welcomed, visitors smile.**

March **is the month of breezy winds, yet we have peace. Hot soup lifts hunger and add spice to our life.**

April **is the month of flowers about to say, hello world you made it through. Colors speak peaceful and free.**

May **is the month of birds chirping ever so softly upon the musical tones of nature. We are at our best.**

June **is the month of dedication, strength and fortitude. For we've come thus far by faith, in God, ourselves and loved ones.**

July **is the month of heat patterns… that have passed this way before. We survived …all one day at a time.**

* *

" Months "

(Part II)

August **is the month of recollection of our thoughts that help others along. Smiles get more bold.**

September **is the month of awareness of character and what we've accomplished up to now.**

October **is the month of harvest of goals, acting quickly for the year's end. Share love, sacrifice time for others.**

November **is the month of our prayerful thanks and promising wishes to come about. To dine is delight.**

December **is the month of end results, dreams, enhanced by the glitter of gifts. We are yet happy.**

"See Where God Leads You, Then Go"

When you're seeking God, be on the
look out for His Word and voice,
The signs will be up everywhere only
look to the hills for your choice.
Vision is a must, then walk in trust.

* *

" A Calendar Of Thought "

For all the *years* you stood by my side
I'm grateful to you, you didn't have to
do any of it...but God sends it through.
You did *years* of hard work just to help
out people like me, you were concerned
about yourself...yet sacrificed it as free.

Then the *months* that you toiled to help
with projects of a kind, you were not...
obligated...it's in your heart and mind.
As *months* went by, you blossomed even
more into a helpful soul, all taught from
relatives from prominent.... days of old.

Along came *days* that...you'd stop by to
counsel and lift my spirit up, you did
chores for others with love in your cup.
At last came *hours* that we touched and
agreed with prayer and praise, knowing
power of words, sincerity...in our ways.

We take a thing one *second* at a time for
it's sometimes needed in that way,
Things can be tough in life, and seconds
would get us through the day.

You've made me stronger by all the help
you sent me as a friend,
And I use it as "A Calendar Of Thought"
for you help me make it in.

* *

" Things You've Done For Me "

I can not even try to count everything
for it has been a lot for me to name,
Simple things, and love you expressed,
yet it means all the same.
Whether it was a gesture, just saying
hello as you ran an errand in need,
Or if it was a kind word to say to me
"Try and you will succeed."

Whether early morning.... when the
sunrise did shine upon my eyes,
Or when the times in life you merely
told me to look toward the skies.
Right now it means so much to me for
you really have touched my heart,
After reminiscing over my life I see
that you gave me a new start.
Steadily you coached me along, saying
things that stayed on my mind,
You knew one day that it'd really take
hold and many joys I would find.

Oh, the peacefulness it brings for me
to have learned a lesson so dear,
All because the Lord sent you this way
and told me what I needed to hear.
Now it's my turn to express how it's
mutually agreed for you to see,
I've learned and progressed from the
many "Things You've Done For Me."

* *

" Myself "

**In reality to reach out to people I see a sense of beauty and love,
For it points to a Higher Being for it's not in my individuality but from above.**

**To reach to the lonely, or make happy thoughts to people as free,
Is what is instilled, and has brought an enhancement to me.**

**To sit alone and think of others, and to pray for their best interest at hand,
It's richness… in my inner being that's here to help me to stand.**

**I seem to… reach out to others that is in need taking the focus off "Myself,"
Someone must step out and help others whilst they have a little faith left.**

**To broaden a sense of self worth it may take "Myself" indeed,
Expressing how I feel about life and how I dearly want to succeed.**

**I'll try to be strong as I now venture on running in tune to life's demands,
I really am the controller of my destiny and the one…who understands.**

* *

" My Friends "

They look for ways to keep a smile upon
my face upon the morn,
For they're concerned about my person
some I've known since I was born,

It's fine that they have other things that
they must dearly do,
Yet, they can take the time to say, "even
though," I still thought of you.

Now, I would be pleased to have these
people around me every day,
For to just look upon their faces puts a
smile in place to stay.

It's such a pleasure for they bring to me
a sincere love at heart,
It remains long after we have conversed
and then depart.

It's a sense of...character not wavering
from a lovely personality trait,
They're very caring people and patiently
upon me wait.

When in need of an extra few minutes of
time for my concern and care,
I know I can count on..."My Friends" to
reach out to me...and to be there.

* *

" One Candle, One Person "

Light a candle whilst you dine, it doesn't
take numbers to make you feel fine.
Realizing that others also have things of
concern, stand the test as you learn.
Pray to the Lord, He hears your request,
Talking to friends as you sincerely confess.

Converse helping each other to be strong,
Confessing to weakness as you all go along.
Walking down the street or in your space,
Think of things you can do to run this race.
You will be refreshed as you start on your
walk, blessing while you and God do talk.

Understanding the way that you should go,
Within your heart getting strength to know.
The Word of God blesses you at every turn,
"One Candle, One Person" you can learn.
Being alone is only a phrase and a state,
Light a candle for yourself, don't you wait.
You can dine and be in... a peaceful light,
"One Candle, One Person" really will be a
sincere delight.

" An Example of An Example "

Look at me and see an example, I look at you and see an example. As we look at each other we see "An Example of An Example" as we live in harmony and peace, love and patience.

* *

" A Candlelight Of Hope "

We are in times of hope for we can have
it within,
As we go on with our life and look to our-
selves as we win.

We can meet with family and friends and
shed some light,
Furthering our freedom to choose and the
marvelous light.

We have the right to hope and be at our
very best,
After all that we have done to help our-
selves along to rest.

We now can be in a state of comfort and
complete calm,
For we need to always trust God and not
be in alarm.

Look to the light of the wholesome sun as
you go through your daily walk,
And view "A Candlelight Of Hope" as you
go through your daily talk.

" A Daily Example "

Removing frowns with smiles will gently supply a day's worth of happiness. It will answer a cry for help, by its steadfastness.

* *

" Encourage Yourself "

When the funds are low and you are
dealing with a concern,
When the market is at a high yet your
yield didn't earn.

When the people are not as pleasant
as you thought,
When times bring cares along with
things you bought.

When the going get tough and it just
seem like it stays,
When you reach to others and they
overlook your good ways.

When you walk hand in hand with a
friend, yet they're not always around,
When you steadily press your way try-
ing to remain sound.

And, when you read God's Word and
you realize He knows how you feel,
Then you can..."Encourage Yourself"
and get back on an even keel.

" Encouraged Daily "

Feeling free, lovely, lively, all because
you have the victory in your heart and
mind, and now it shows on your face.

* *

" Encourage Your Friends "

Whether by day or by night, they don't
really have to walk alone,
For you can reach out to them by mail
or a visit, computer or phone.

Whether it last for a day, or an hour it
would be for their benefit,
For you can say to them nice things and
be ever so close knit.

Whether you tell them your trials to.....
strengthen and brighten their day,
For they can look at your life's victories
too and go on their way.

Whether you build them to a state that
they really deserve,
For they can be drawn to your goodness
and how you daily serve.

Whether it's distant or near, you can
always lend a helpful hand,
For if you..."Encourage Your Friends"
they may in turn help you to stand.

" Encourage All "

If they lend a smile or two, or say nice
things, send it back today. If they don't,
send it anyway, and expect...a miracle.

* *

" The Ease Of Prayer "

When we humble ourselves to talk to the Lord as we begin to kneel,
We bring to Him our cares, requesting help, He knows how we feel.

He's a Higher Being, yet touched by our words of a sincere heart and mind,
As we pray in the spirit, the intercession is made of words we can't find.

Oftentimes, we venture to pray for our loved ones yet leaving out oneself,
All the time thinking we will be counted in the number of the blessings that's left.

But sometimes we search for the good and try to see God in everything,
Looking to Him for forgiveness and return others the familiar ring.

It's as easy as talking to our family, our co-workers, or a friend,
All we have to do is open our hearts and let the Lord sincerely in.

So now we open our mouths and let…"The Ease Of Prayer" be expressed,
For it's just as easy as….our words to our friends that's truly blessed.

* *

" The Ease Of Praise "

It doesn't take a lot to praise God for
His goodness that He shows,
For it's all worth the blessing that we
all receive as faith grows.

We press to say to the Lord that He's a
good God all the time, all the love,
He allows us to share time with others a
true blessing sent from above.

He takes us through trials and keeps us
at our best in days of victorious tests,
For we come through triumphantly and
it's not because we've done our best.

The Lord gets the glory and it all belong
right there in the first place,
No waiting to experience joyful times in
this wonderful Christian race.

The Lord is just good and the joy can't
be summed up with many words or few,
For the Word of God tells us He has....
unspeakable joy, found in me and you.

" Praise and Honour "

God deserves all the praise we can give
Him and more beside, He doesn't need
us, we need Him to keep up the stride.

* *

" The Aftermath Of Suffering "

Rest gloriously, and wisely for you have won the fight,
Just because of opinions it doesn't make them right.

When you walk in the daytime walk with faith in your heart,
When you rest at night, smile, and know you've won from the start.

It's not like, you haven't been there before and did not embark,
On a mission where you didn't back up in midstream but put it in park.

You then can regroup and get a second wind on your side,
Then you will put your life in gear and enjoy the ride.

Be tough, relax more, let the concerns ease away,
"The Aftermath Of Suffering"...means that you didn't in it stay.

" Don't Accept It "

If it dampens your spirit, if it sounds untoward God, if it doesn't uplift you, it doesn't show love, "Don't Accept It."

* *

" The Joy Of Suffering "

**It feels like a little discomfort for most
people like a life of ease,
Some people are just accustomed to not
getting involved, doing as they please.**

**Happiness isn't always in the easy things
in life at hand,
Because it's sometime the tough things
that build you up to stand.**

**You can make your stand even though
the going is dim it seems,
When you focus your mind on the Lord
and let your light really beam.**

**Who would get a release just by accept-
ing victory through it all,
For the quickness of faith makes your
very concerns, seem small.**

**We all know that the Lord, will be with
us, in whatever for Him we do,
And, also should know that "The Joy Of
Suffering"...brings blessings down on you.**

" Count It As Victory "

**When things seems to not go your way,
accept victory in the Lord to defend, for
how things turn out, will on Him depend.**

* *

" A Lover Of Poems "

Could we say a lot by saying words flow
with power in a line,
When we read the words over and over
until it really is fine.

It seems to grab a hold of our attention
as we rest from today's labor,
When we give space for reading casually
we do ourselves a favor.

Especially, when we find time to read a
portion of God's Divine Word every day,
For it'll certainly suffice our daily need
of encouragement in a spiritual way.

We get through trials, as we look at how
others have been blessed,
For it's for our very example so that we
are able to get some rest.

In the natural sense we read, all over the
course of a day, a great book,
And we see by the example of others what
it really took.

To be "A Lover Of Poems" will be a great
thing in life to obtain,
For it will help erase the concerns and be
...for your very gain.

* *

" A Lover Of Kind Words "

Of course all things will not be for us to
understand in our heart,
But we need to keep the joy of happiness
within as we start.

We can lift people up and build up many
blessed people to win,
Also we can administer our services to be
like family and kin.

It's not too much to say things to make a
person feel free,
When we're "A Lover Of Kind Words"
it's easy for us to see.

The enhancement of a person's ease of
mind as found in you and me,
Will be a help for someone as their path
in life come to be.

For it will put us on a spiritual high and
bring us to another level of desire,
When we realize that the Lord gets the
glory from what we now admire.

"A Lover Of Kind Words" brings a lovely
relationship to our feelings within,
For when we spread the goodness of God
to others, we build up a friend.

* *

" To Reach A Friend "

As we sort through a lot of things in life
we learn lessons from a school,
After we get stronger we learn it was the
school of hard knocks as a rule.

For what we didn't learn as an example
we had to in a hard way,
When oftentimes, the words of parents
seemed to fall and not stay.

Oh yes, it gets real busy when we try to
tell others how to live,
All by the life we express, with our love
as we give.

Now we can give an example pressing on
to fulfill the dream,
Take along someone with you and it will
be like a team.

The better way to do things will be to have
a compassionate heart,
In the meanwhile it will be a very blessing
on your part.

In order to appear to be kind, you must
touch someone with your heart,
And, in order "To Reach A Friend"...you
must certainly, make a start.

* *

" To Understand A Friend "

You don't really have to stay with them
night and day to learn of their ways,
For your presence will be ever with them
on rainy or sunny days.

From your reaching out to your friends
they feel like next of kin,
By your soft tone of voice, they know that
on your side, they will win.

For you will listen with your ears, yet
your heart will do better,
Speaking peace to your neighbor in all
seasons and weather.

You look out your window, the sunshine
seem to speak to you,
And it's the way it is with your friends...
in everything you do.

Now your friends look to you, so remain
strong, you can help out,
When life presses upon their door you can
help relieve the doubt.

You can be a real blessing to them if a....
kindness is expressed,
That's a way "To Understand A Friend"
and help them do their best.

* *

" We Walk Hand In Hand "

**Most of our lives we are a way for others
to be happy and feel free,
We sometimes never meet in the course
of the day, but on our knee.**

**That's when we pray for each other and
we feel the prayers go up,
Never knowing sometimes that strangers
pray love into our cup.**

**We feel the warmth of God's love as we
kneel down to pray,
Praying for our fellowman to go success-
fully on their way.**

**All friends do not have a tolerance for all
of our concerns,
But a chosen few will standby you as the
prayer wheel turns.**

**You speak a word or two and who knows
how it will fill a heart with joy,
Oftentimes the words reaches with love to
whom it will employ.**

**Be a keeper of pleasant themes.... to pass
along, to help someone to stand,
And know that when we do show kindness
...and love "We Walk Hand In Hand."**

* *

" We Talk A Language Of Love "

You are so nice, did you hear that on a
day when you needed it the most?
Even though you might not have heard
it you can in the Lord boast.

For the Lord will send you somebody
don't fret yourself over the thought,
He always has sent someone along with
what life has brought.

For that someone will coach you and
be by your very side,
In so doing, they will help you to take
life's concerns in stride.

You are so nice, did you hear that on a
night when you needed to relax?
For it would have helped you to live
victoriously to the max.

Hooray for the trials for they will come
as being in the plan,
Hallelujah to them anyhow for God will
give us the victory as seen in the land.

Reach to God asking for a blessed word
from above,
And it will be manifested in our lives as
..."We Talk A Language Of Love."

* *

" When Your Friend Is Young "

**You know young people, can express a
thing or two into existence,
Led by the Hand of God, as they use a
spirit of persistence.**

**"When Your Friend Is Young," please
remember a birthday, or important day,
For they would do the same for you and
send you happily on your way.**

**People love to be thought of from a view-
point of thoughtful ways,
When they get older they will more than
likely, reminisce as it stays.**

**It will be a dear reminder of your great
compassion for them long ago,
For all they know, they didn't expect the
things you said to really show.**

**Their minds are yet young, but you can
through kindness win their favor,
For you are perhaps next door or if far
yet treat them like a neighbor.**

**These young people will remember you
and race to your arms to embrace,
"When Your Friend Is Young," help is
needed, for they have the world to face.**

* *

" When Your Friend Is Older "

**We all will come along in life with our
meaningful fulfillment and goals,
When we were young for the most part
the half had not been told.
We rush through life, sometimes not
realizing the older heads as wise,
As they look upon the windowsills and
see the sunlight arise.
These people know what they're talk-
ing about, as they tell you how to do,
So you don't have to suffer the many
consequences, that may come to you.**

**So "When Your Friend Is Older" keep
them in mind and visit them or call,
For they thought of you when you were
a child and only small.
Even if you didn't know them earlier it
matters not when passing a test,
For you're glad to get reliable advice
and get through the rest.**

**We could be farther along as we step
out in life and be bolder,
Yet remembering where it came from...
even "When Your Friend Is Older."
Let them know you care for them even
if you just met them sometimes ago,
For they've been down the road you're
traveling... so believe that they know.**

* *

" Forever In My Heart "

My friend you are such a comfort to me
and I appreciate your ways,
You lift my spirit to a level, that I have
many happy days.

Just to think of your kindness seems to
give me a second wind,
When I think of all the goodness, and
that God sent you to me, as a friend.

You didn't just happen to blow into my
life, as it was in the plan,
For it's truly amazing how the Lord has
so much love for our fellowman.

He in turn takes His love and gives it to
us to help ease our walk,
You my friend have done a very good
thing, to include me in your talk.

I feel the love my friend, that now flows
through the universe from your smile,
As hope of your presence stays peaceful
and lingers on for a great while.

For when I think of family, I think also
of you, my dear precious friend,
Though we met as strangers, I will keep
you "Forever In My Heart" as we win.

* *

" Forever, My Friend "

We can express our gratitude by many
gestures, in essence of peace,
We can show love by actions and standby
whilst concerns decrease.
We can reach out to a stranger and say a
kind word expressing love,
We can go to another level and get more
encouragement from above.
We can be like a strong fortress and say
to our friend "Be strong,"
We can be blessed and understood as we
give praises to God in song.

We can know that God knows everything
that will ever come our way,
For He will send what we need to get us
through, on any given day.

We can say "Friend, you're a beacon light
sent to accompany me,"
We can reach out to heaven and focus our
heart to be free.
We can be blessed, when friends come our
way to help spread a smile or two,
For we also can visit our friends, and assist
them as they venture through.
We can fully hope in God's love that will be
forever there, throughout eternity,
We can also strive to let it be "Forever, My
Friend" ...found in you and me.

There's strength and the wonderful feeling of friendship in the air, and hearts, as you mellow out with family, friends....in a state of love. Living is a continuous part in life, it goes further by friendship, and every day in encouragement draws hearts together as one.

Being that people converse daily without a major awakening, it brings a closer bond to all. Giving a little of ourselves, will reinforce fellowship of...*"The Ring Of Friends: Forever,"* and we all.... will be in a state of growth, and freedom for a perpetual time. Advice is good, whether heard or not...for let it at least be said that "We tried."

What an expression of love we have in life with friends......that we can encounter and hold on to with aspiration.

For this one instance....I have a personal story whereby, I will withhold names, but ...tell you of my experience. On the job.... with the Feds upon leaving, I was asked, if I would depart from my desk pad. It was scribbled on, with short strokes of red ink, all arrayed, on green poster board. It was used to protect the desk, from stray marks of such red ink.

What the essence, of this denotes is...this just so happened to be, a famous desk pad that held memories, scriptures.....of course also some of my sayings. For the scriptures it had an assortment.....No weapon formed against me shall prosper...and others.

There is no wisdom nor understanding nor counsel against the Lord. For my sayings...Say No More, Just Give It To Jesus ...In Due Time...and others. Anyway, this desk pad was a conversation piece, like no other. The request couldn't be granted for I had tossed it to the large file thirteen,.... and little did I know, that it had already been retrieved by another co-worker, they were ecstatic and so enthused.

I felt like sounding off, all the way to the top of my inspired lungs...to have someone to try and hold on to memories of me, my person, even by ways of a desk pad that I'd used constantly for about three years at the most, of my ten years with the Feds.

I lit up to the Lord, and said "Lord Jesus, I thank you, that I have at least touched.... someone's mind, and heart with Your love and Your Word."

Such dedication from friends......and the farewell luncheon was rated as superb. It was a great send-off...with my daughter as a great planner, of the event, along with a few other friends. I highly treasure it to ... this moment...these wonderful friends. I remember them by revisiting them, every ...now and again.

This is about caring people, and friends that has always been there, for me, and I feel so privileged, and ecstatic, about their genuine nature, and love towards me. The freedom, in friendships...speaks for itself.

* *

America's Victory After The Attack September 11, 2001 Bringing A Closure For America ...Dedicated to The Lost, Victims, Survivors and Person of The Year 2001: Mayor Rudolph W. Giuliani, New York Also to: Governor George Pataki, New York

Many have tried to survive, and bring closure to what has been a challenge upon America. Many are surviving with the help of God, and then family, friends, ministers, churches, fire fighters, police, medics, news media, FBI, the CIA, and a host of others, also fine general communities, fine dedicated people, of these United States of America...United We Stand.

I sincerely hope that these poems will be read in love, and peaceful harmony. I've tried to spare any discomfort, I hope, I've succeeded. I will talk about the strength, unity, the very devotion of people, all over the world, and the ones, directly involved...in this event that has left many without words to say...we can try.

Yet faith, their steadfastness in a Great God, of mercy, love, peace...has brought them thus far, and certainly will take them into a realm where they can find...solace and closure.

You Are Welcomed Here As Friends... as Family, it is hoped that these poems will most certainly be a blessing to you.

"The Ring Of Friends: Forever" - *Florence Rosie Givens*

* *

" Our Right "

Amidst the stars, stripes and sea, we do stand tall, all of the glory to God in the midst of us all.
Be it freely, or be it a fight, we all stand united with our might.

We refuse to bow under such a weighted task, when protection of our country we duly ask. Be it freely or be it a fight, our homeland "*America*".....is "Our Right."

" In America, Our Rights "

On September 11, 2001;
Uncalled things were done.
Right here in our homeland;
Rivaling us to make a stand.
In a time of freedom's ring;
God Bless America we sing.
Here is how it all will end;
Touch America we'll defend.
Surely victory, we have won;
...Since, September 11, 2001.

" We've Won "

We have the victory, we are
strong in faith, and in words.
Our richness, states victory...
the track record...yet stands.

* *

" Opinions "

It's now of our obvious, and observant sight,
That things sometimes are not at all so right.
It makes for a deliberate, a devastating state,
And has now brought on less love more hate.
We're now in a natural, and spiritual sense,
We're here on earth, must live however tense.
Senses, phases, in all the times at best today,
Pray that the President, go dearly on his way.

The job's given him of our Country to defend,
To fly the proud American Flag, and now win.
Keep the prayers flowing, and be really upbeat,
To grasp the time, that doesn't bring on defeat.
We will think of things we now see clear at last,
From a very dear hindsight of our historic past.
Be it right to us, or be it wrong, do fly the Flag,
Not being a wagon rider who grumbles and lag.
The American Flag, that is, to my recollection,
Is the Flag, of our solid, American's collection.

It matters not mainly what we really say or do,
If it's not meant to be of all .... "Opinions" too.
Respect the many wishes of others and cherish,
All the goodwill, they do, and not let it perish.
You've spoken your mind, and others will too,
It's their "Opinions" of how they get through.
One day, they will hopefully realize their state,
Of their "Opinions" as we now, solemnly wait.
Keep support going on, to our people at hand,
God Bless our "Opinions"...America our Land.

* *

" An Umbrella For America "

**Hopefully, with your stars, stripes, keep me,
All the whilst now history comes to divert me.
I know that you're there for me and the land,
I know you're for the Nation to understand.**

**You keep me dry when the rains of life befall,
You keep me uplifted all of these years so tall.
I want to say to you now what is your name?
We all are under you and we're all the same.**

**It's for the Nation, that you are now, in to be,
A comfort to many people, and comfort to me.
Now tell me your name, for I can not guess,
For the people are either talking, or confess.**

**You keep us warm, dry, you're over our head,
You try to be in the front lines not us instead.
Tell me what is your name, the answer awaits?
"I'm The American Flag of The United States."
"An Umbrella For America" I'm really called,
Liberty, justice...pursuit of happiness to all.**

" A Rose For America "

**May your hearts be uplifted and strength-
ened by God's love, an everlasting hope and
steadfast grace from above.
Look ever to God, for it's far past our own
wisdom and sight, yet to go on with "A Rose
For America".... at this time seems right.**

* *

" Reaching You "

(Part I)

Yesterdays and yesteryears, have been
running through my mind,
I reach for your touch, your comfort is
what I now find.

I know that it seems tough for me to go
through this stage,
Yet it's worth it all to me, for the ease
will come with age.

I grasp the time and say to myself "Hold
on dear soul,"
For you wouldn't want me to just sit here
and not in life behold.

I mean to behold the beauty and the array
of hope that you have set,
Whilst our hearts and minds touched as...
you were still as yet.

And now it brings me to this time in life
that a moment passes quickly too,
For I cherish how in the universe I'm able
to grasp a picture of you.

Even though it's tough I'm still thankful
for my heart's closure in peace,
For one day, you were there for me and
your love will never cease.

* *

" Reaching You "

(Part II)

A closure of harmony, even though you
have now moved on,
I feel warmth in my heart and will now
reunite with you on the morn.

All I really have to do is now reach out
and feel my spirit anew,
And in so doing this...act of kindness I
will be "Reaching You."

Of course it's in my heart and mind, in
quietness and in hope,
For the moments of kind caring ways of
others help me to cope.

How can it be done? When can it be done?
Can it really be done to make a whole?
To pull together myself, to go on with my
life, and every day to be bold?

Yes I can, yes I will, for I have much help
within myself,
For I will grasp a hold of faith, and all the
integrity, that I, still have left.

" Survival Within "

I wish to reach the dreams I hold dear. As,
I listen to my heart's integrity very steadily,
I also hear the Lord answering me, readily.

* *

" In My Heart, I Touch You "

Hidden deep in my heart I guess I could really say,
That I long to press over hurdles on each given day.

A walk along the way keeping you always as a part of me,
And "In My Heart, I Touch You" and it... seems to set me free.

" Life's Closure "

You were there, and I knew that it was in life so grand,
You were a great peace to me and together we did stand.

Yet now I search to comfort myself and... others along the way,
With "Life's Closure" of your kindness as it will always stay.

"Amidst The Harmony "

I've found and cherished times of our love,
I've reached to peaceful things as the dove.
I search, for you, and my heart has found,
Peace "Amidst The Harmony"......around.

* *

" Be Brave "

Broaden your chest amidst the storms,
Days will come along, out of the norm.
You'll stand firm and you will behold,
Say now, "Be Brave" as you were told.

"Strengthen Your Heart"

Be quiet, be strong, you will make it
all the way through,
You have others around you to be of
comfort to you.

Do all you can for yourself, and then for
others do your part,
In so doing this deed to help others you
too will "Strengthen Your Heart."

" But For A Moment "

All of it is worth it, stay focused and
and keep yourself free,
Continue on in your faith and then you
will grow as the tree.

Even if it passes over you, it will be yet
still grand,
That you... even "But For A Moment"
made your stand.

Staying encouraged always...surviving life.

* *

" United We Stand "

For love, for health, for freedom as it ring,
Together we forgive, but remember a thing.
How we were shaken in this now solemn land.
Yet it profited us, so it's "United We Stand."

" Bravely "

The fire fighters, health officials, police, and
Mayor Giuliani, and Governor Pataki too,
Were there and are still there in their hearts
yet heartily, serving you.
Should it be the bravery of the color purple,
I dearly think so,
For they with Mayor Giuliani's, Governor
Pataki's, and other's help, yet "Bravely" go.

" Courageously "

All of the firefighters, police and health care
members were there, they showed solemnly
that they did really, sincerely care.
Time goes on for the Pentagon, our military
base of power, as they "Courageously" go on
with many duties at any given hour.

" You Are Remembered "

To all who helped, who did suffice, all who
paid the price. Our hearts are daily reaching
out, "You Are Remembered" without a doubt.

" The Twin Towers, New York City "

Phantom feelings of you being there in the
power and the light,
As we look forward to you into the depth
of time through the night.

We can accomplish what we strongly urge
and have set out to do, with a sort of kind
remembrance, and to now follow it through.

To build in your space, a place of elevation
of our solemn pride,
For we will keep you in our hearts, and....
forever walk in pride.

" The Pentagon, Washington, DC "

The force and tower of power resting on our
American soil,
Has been enhanced by the men and women
and all who toil.

To keep our country free, and in the pursuit
of harmony and peace,
To press to reach the goals until this course
of disharmony cease.

Of strength you stand, and cover a broad...
compassion of love and goodwill,
Set in accordance with standards, you yet
remain there still.

* *

" Manhattan, NY, Stands Abroad "

**Amidst trials and storms of life solemn
faced heroes, of Manhattan, NY, stood,
Snow capped buildings now months later
hindered not the progress, that it could.
High talking newscasters spread the then
news in lands of near and foreign soil,
Yet, pressed the workers of Manhattan,
NY, for they let not up on the toil.**

**Day and night tiresomely, softheartedly
workers drenched in water of their pores,
Wrestling with heartaches and the times
that now press upon their doors.
Believe them to be heroes in Manhattan,
NY, you've seen them in fervent action,
As they ready the city for visitors and the
pertinent worldly attraction.**

**Tis, amidst the struggles that these people
gathered more strength within their heart,
Determined to pull together for Manhattan,
NY, certainly did their individual part.
Oh yes, Manhattan, NY, stood the test and
pressed upon times beyond their control,
And so we see a proud part of New York as,
"Manhattan, NY, Stands Abroad," as of old.
A keeper of the encouragement, a steadfast...
team in search of hopeful victory in its place,
Oh yes, after seeing all that we did see, we
know that Manhattan, NY, keeps...its pace.**

* *

" A Proud New York "

How proud should a City be to be called
a City of Strength laid upon the ground,
As you look, to the height of it, and then
back down and around.
Did you see all the prosperity that draped
the famous New York, City?
Oh, the boroughs, and the precincts, oh,
they don't want the pity.
Tis, for but a season and New York City
will be more at its best,
Whilst tourists and onlookers break the
ribbons of the test.

How proud, then could New York be...
after what it's been through,
Tell that to a New Yorker, oh no, not to
let it be a thought from you.
You should know that this City is strong,
with chests as a forward stance,
Reminded of the hopes and dreams and
how the avenues dance.

Oh, they will dance again alongside our
America's courageous faithful few,
As they open the Theaters with live plays
for then tourists can see the view.
And the sum of "A Proud New York"...
can't be counted on your hand,
For it's made up of a lot of people all of
a wonderful proud land.

* *

" New York Today "

After September 11, 2001 we look at
New York and its strong resolve,
We press over issues and we still have
things yet to solve.
Push and shove will be the words in a
gentle caring way of life for them,
For it's what it took of their hearts to
then stay above the rim.
They were pushed on that day in time
in September to a limit they only knew,
The outcome of their faith impressed
and also encouraged you.
They had to go on their way, and they
received help from abroad and near,
Not then having time for petty concerns
and neither the realm of fear.
They brushed off their knees, put then
shovels in hand, and prayed,
Everyone pulled together, draped in...
lovely ways, as they stayed.
Oh, they stayed connected and put on
an extra layer of love, they reached to
get some help from the Lord up above.
Imagine what the people of New York
would've done if they weren't strong,
You look at "New York Today"...and
say it didn't take them that long.
Rebuild the City rebuild the hope, and
the strength that makes you all cope.
"God Bless, New York."

* *

" As You Think Of New York "

Yes, you may give to New York your
poor, your rich, they will suffice,
Of all the people in this world you need
not have mention twice.

Off shore they're great with the many
skyscrapers to test your will,
Visit New York, in the essence of the
land, they stand ready still.

You can reach out to the universe yet
find them a character great in ease,
On the off shores of your life, standing
at New York Harbor, if you please.

Dressed in apparel that tells you of the
tourist attractions and Broadway,
The mayor beckons you to the City of
New York every day.

Of course you will benefit and feel you
have done your part,
"As You Think Of New York" and give
them the kindness of your heart.

" I Love New York "

New York City is enriched with many
people in all walks of life, sports lovers,
electrifying the stadium.......with love.

* *

" Pennsylvania's Hope "

A part of September 11, 2001, touched upon your soil,
Yet your name may not have been called out much in the toil.

Someone though thought to let you know we care about you,
And a part of America also fell upon the hearts that you have too.

We're praying for your strength in...... Pennsylvania as we are for New York, and Washington, DC,
We hear your cry of love and all the.... compassion you give as free.

Now the Governor of Pennsylvania and its people deserve praise,
When New York, and Washington, DC joined in you did too your arms raise.

You all raised them in victory that was fresh upon every morn,
As the newscasters spoke of the act that on Pennsylvania's land was born.

Now it's a fact that you, Pennsylvania was included as one that did cope,
And we want to be included in with you ....and "Pennsylvania's Hope."

* *

" A Touch Of Love "

**New York, Washington, DC, Pennsylvania,
and let's include Virginia, for they were all
on the news report,
With a devastated time at hand everyone yet
pulled then together of a sort.**

**There were no barriers for love washed them
away, on the way to Cathedrals they stopped
along the way to pray.**

**They went into the churches and held each...
other closely by embrace,
Knowing that it took strength to get through
what they had to face.**

**Then the people made a place of refuge for...
loved ones to meet,
Pressing upon hearts to be strong, to hold...
fast and stand upon their feet.**

**Boldly these people pulled together, and ...
together they had soft smiles,
And "A Touch Of Love" rained upon their
hearts and got them over the miles.**

**People have love in these United States of
America and a kindred of others to be,
And on that day of September 11, 2001 it...
proved that love was found in you and me.**

* *

" Carry The Torch "

For the brave souls, that had the courage to rescue, and protect us. For the timeframe of work that was enhanced by love, for our America.

For the many that left but were not forgotten and will live in our hearts. For the many hearts, that will take part in events, even though they're not present, but are in far lands.

For the longing that is expressed in hearts because of absence of their... loved ones, family, and friends. For the remembrance of the Nation for which we stand in America.

Doing this and more as time heals concerns, you'll "Carry The Torch" with a proud face and a smile knowing that together...United We Stand.
God Bless America, America Bless God.

The visit here was hopefully of help,
do read this portion of poetry again.
Please remember that we do change
...but the Lord never does... never!
You can't be everything, just be you.
"The Ring Of Friends: Forever" -Florence Rosie Givens

* *

" Get An Uplift "

Whether you get a friendly hello
or a word of cheer,
You must go on and get enthused
and get out of here.
Things don't just stop and not go
on its way,
So it gives us time to know what
we're going to say.
Also things are not as permanent
as heaven is for us,
So know this calls for a lot of the
real genuine trust.

We do find this trust in the Lord,
He won't lead you astray,
For when you trust Him mightily
He sends blessings your way.
Of course we need some blessings
every day for a good measure,
Then the things like unto God are
the things we do treasure.

What we need right now is a nice
fellowship with family or friend,
And hope that they are grounded
in the Word of God to the end.
Yet if you don't get encouragement
turn to the Lord with smiles,
For He is the one who matters, He's
the one who gets us over the miles.

Now that you've read to a near conclusion in this book *"The Ring Of Friends: Forever"* you may say "It was nice, wonderful, good," let it not stop there... care and share it with your loved ones and friends.

Encourage your friends to get an uplift, a release on life; share it as a gift to them... that they may also feel the presence of love and friendship through words of poetry.

When something in life is pleasant, we'd like to share it...most definitely. Share the love of God with family, and friends and share this book......*"The Ring Of Friends: Forever"* and the likes of it, in *"A Morning Without Coffee"* and, *"Revisiting Friends: The Journey Home."* The three, are a real compilation of poems, that your library... should have at home or in the office, for a few moments of comfort in your life when needed....for yourself or to share with the people in your life....that you, are fond of.

Poetry here, is in every day language..... each poem has a story to tell...who knows if it will touch your life, as a road that you have traveled or yet will travel. Let it be a source of kindness to you, be good to yourself, ponder points of interest, use a bookmark to arrive back at your favorite poem or selected reading...jot the page down.

Life holds wonderful keys to our dreams and happiness, some find it in all facets of life, family, friends, work, business, yet let it be found... in our hearts.

Of course, we search for a story or some moral point in life, that has a stay upon... our minds...find it here, as you now read on and find the poems to be about life, and the reality of the...matter at hand. Only to believe, starts us on a road of triumphant especially when we believe in God and then in friendship, and ourselves.

Let us be gifted with a gaining effect...as we venture to lands and avenues of life that is comforting and pleasant. Go walking, go running, jogging, to movies, ball games, all types of sports with friends...go to Fenway Park, Fed Ex Field, cheer on the New York Yankees, the New York Mets...or a team... of your choice. Just...standby your friends.

We are a very diversified people, and we have feelings that we want respected, lifted, pampered, and we can start by showing the love that we in return want. It was a very... mere thought to begin writing about people and about life...when this Poetry book idea surfaced, along with the Author's idea that to be uplifted is to be closer to God.

We can be closer to God by our sincerity, by our dedication, steadfastness, and a deep love for the Word of God, in our hearts, our minds, and walking daily in fellowship with Him, and with all people, of all nationalities and races. Yes, love has no colors...poetry should neither have colors, but if it must be expressed, yet find words of love to express it...it will make a better world, and life too.

* *

" The Five Community Mothers "

(Part I)

They all live in a small town, somewhere in the world. They have a bond of love... and character that the many people and neighbors awaits.
Now the *first* one, is the strongest of the five, yet the others draw love from her... caring ways,
They gather together to clean houses and prepare dinner for people for many days.
The *second* one, gathers the chicken then set out to meet within the hour,
The *third* one, carries a bag of green beans to prepare, for she has the power.
The *fourth* one, sprinkles the clothes with the sprinkler as she pray,
The *fifth* one, live in the vicinity, and will get picked up on the way.

Now the *first* one, has gathered clothes to give to neighbors also food galore,
While the *second* one, mops the floor as she looks to the Dear Lord all the more.
Other food choices, are purchased then are prepared at the main house of their choice,
The *third* one, rushes to be of assistance yet listening and using her voice.
The *fourth* one, says to the ladies, after this we will dearly move on,
The *fifth* one, knew all of these other ladies when they were born.

* *

" The Five Community Mothers "

(Part II)

All of these Mothers get together as they
then sweep through the neighborhood,
Feeling free, to be what the Lord wants
them to be, and dearly distributing food.

They all gather together for prayer that
they learned about a long time ago,
And they know the power of prayer for
their parents let them know.

That in order, to receive their blessings
they must spread goodwill and cheer,
So these *five* Mothers, do put away their
feelings, and then sacrifice so dear.

People love these Mothers and call them
each by their last name,
Had not the Lord sent these *five* dear....
Mothers it would not be the same.

All *five* of them always do their very best
helping others and themselves to live,
For they with their innermost being reach
out to the community and give.

Now they look for nothing in return for...
God put goodness and love in their heart,
We should be like "The Five Community
Mothers"... making it true from the start.

* *

" The Five Community Mothers "

(Part III)

From house to house they go, spreading the blessings of the realness of their goals,
For these *five* Mothers fast and pray, reaching out to where life has taken its tolls.

They know of the responsibility and try to be pleasant in everything they do,
For these *five* Mothers of this community have a family as well as you.

Yet, they share their time and worth and whisper not a word of their deed,
For God has blessed them to be mourning women, spreading cheer to those in need.

(In the poem "The Five Community Mothers" All names, places are fictitious and are not related to real people or circumstances, coincidence, or events.) -Florence Rosie Givens

" The Old Way, The Good Paths "

This is a true story and here is the way it used to be and it now goes, years ago we would meet at houses for Bible Study and had to stay on our toes. For even though... they served cookies and then something to drink, we yet had to know the Bible verses so our little minds had to study and think.

* *

" What It Is To Be A Mother "

To be a Mother you must be very patient
and yes, wait for God's guidance in life,
Even if it only comes from the little sons
and the daughters, yes, keep down strife.

To be a Mother you must take good care
of your children, giving a roof overhead,
When the time comes, for your freedom
you must sacrifice, and see what's instead.

To be a Mother you must be good to your
children, give needs, a few wants in the cup,
To be a Mother you will probably sacrifice,
will wait, also until the children grow up.

" What It Is To Be A Father"

To be a Father, yes, here it comes, the same
thing again, you thought it was solved,
You should know now that the children are
always thinking things around you revolved.

To be a Father you sometimes allow them
their way and to let them learn a few things,
For the head of a child is not all into the *no*
word but they like how the sound of *yes* rings.

To be a Father takes a lot of God's guidance
and a lot of prayer from you, and like others
you'd sacrifice waiting until school's through.

* *

" The Five Community Fathers "

(Part I)

These community Fathers live in a small
town somewhere in the world we know,
For these men in the community live and
spread blessings as they go.

Now they step out on the lawn and gear up
for the goals of the day,
All *five* of them look not to themselves but
they bow their heads and pray.

Now they know that it will take prayer for
these Fathers try to do what they're told,
It's good to honor and acknowledge God
as in the days of old.

The *first* one, knows the power in being at
their best teaching others the way,
The *second* one, calls the others to remind
them of deeds they will do the next day.

The *third* one, knowing the mechanic duties
blessing the neighborhood with expertise,
The *fourth* one, reaching out as a carpenter
fix what he must, until the problem cease.

The *fifth* one, dearly keeps the tab and they
split the price of the jobs without a rhyme,
Whilst they journey through a community
being brilliant, keeping up with the time.

* *

" The Five Community Fathers "

(Part II)

Sometimes they give elderly people a lift
to get groceries, do chores that's at hand,
Sometimes all *five* community Fathers as
a group show people how to stand.

Some of the things that's done are not....
major jobs to any of them at all,
For they all *five* chip in and it now makes
each other's job very small.

Just to go sit on the porch and hear what
their neighbors had to say,
Will most certainly enhance the owners
and send them on their way.

It won't be long before these Fathers set
an example of their goals at best,
For other people will look to them for...
strength as they pass their test.

Just for these Fathers to be there showing
God in their dear hearts and minds,
Will be all the searchers for God's Word
and His goodness dearly finds.

We all know that "The Five Community
Fathers" should be a thing that's true,
For if you're in the running for a miracle
it could be dearly you.

* *

" The Five Community Fathers "

(Part III)

When all *five* of the community Fathers
starts out they go in prayer,
Knowing that they should acknowledge
God and that He will meet them there.
From days of old these Fathers with a
richness in minds, hearts geared in love,
Have succeeded in their endeavors for
they have been blessed of God above.
They neither look for pay or pat on the
back for things they do,
But walk blessed of the Lord.... so they
bring blessings to their family too.

(In the poem "The Five Community Fathers" All names, places are fictitious and are not related to real people or circumstances, coincidence, or events.) -Florence Rosie Givens

" The Richness Of Guidance "

It's always good to have a wise person in
your clear direct view, for look at all the
times you needed help to get you through.
It's not always that way and we know we
sometimes must just go on,
We reach out to the wisdom that we were
told by others on the morn.
That's why it's good to carry a tablet or...
write it upon our mind, for when we really
need help it won't be so hard for us to find.

* *

" What A Mother Means "

A Mother means that you will get mostly what you want,
It doesn't always mean that it will all be really up front.

It might just come to you after time has dearly past,
Yet if you continue to press it upon her mind it won't last.

For a Mother will go out her way to see you get your need,
And "What A Mother Means" to us will be with us indeed.

" What A Father Means "

A Father means that you could have your way when you ask for help,
All the while you think in your mind and he bought it as you slept.

He might not tell you that he's going to buy it helping along the way,
A Father sometimes let it be a surprise but it on his mind stay.

A Father means you will have security and he will include you in as his friend, yet he'll give guidance, and your rights he'll defend.

"*Life's Little Patient Messages*" No. 1

Bits and pieces of conversations are heard, amongst friends.... as I sat at a restaurant I looked around me, and saw silver-haired patrons. All of them distinguished, with looks of satisfaction, as if they were weathering a storm. Years have a way of bringing us to... grip with life, however tough. Few had looks of amazement, others with proud looks as if a stranger would never be their friend.

For the most part our friends were former strangers before we conversed with them. A sound of voices arrayed the restaurant with a noise of friendship, perhaps...... even foes.

The atmosphere fades out to a few broken sentences, from patrons that frequent there. One older silver-haired couple, never really said a word to each other but stared. Then a silence was broken by the husband's request for a drink refill.....the wife looks at her cup and said, "You want some more?"...he never answered but looked on, as if he'd answered.

Knowing what each other's needs are, ... I guess, is enough for the fulfillment in life. The voices of a newer crowd builds up and I leave, satisfied, refreshed and of...a stronger bond. Sitting there, with strangers- who one day...may be a friend.

In this little message, it goes to show that... people have a need.... to be together to work, play, dine, yet remain in sincere peace, love, harmony, that makes us unique, pleasant, as we're on our way...observing life in serenity.

"Life's Little Patient Messages" No. 2

At this one restaurant I find myself now listening to Country music, played over the speakers universally throughout the restaurant. A few voices here, are mingled and a child's voice is heard, as I reminisce over... my life, in hopes of staging a reality check.

The stage is set, I'm glad to be yet alive, and no matter what comes my way I feel a sense of being as I blend in. I'm part of this vast universe, because God says so...and as I write He speaks to my heart in love. I do have a right to be here, to be happy, to be free. Voices now rise, up to mere maximum and drops to a near silence, as the patrons finish the meals, laughter, giggles and glee.

Life is really great, whatever the state, as I sink into the love of the Lord, His mercies, and great care, I drift also...into His solemn peace. I now, slightly hear music, as other patrons come in. I barely get a real glimpse of their shadows as they pass by me.

The waitress continues smiles of courtesy, and life goes on with all. I've always had a... sense of solitude, so being here alone fares well for me- there's nothing missing here, I have only to look within my heart. Be a .... friend to yourself, thereby you can build up a feeling to be someone else's.... real friend.

A baby now says "hi" to someone as I exit and am now feeling touched by the Hand of God- for whilst sitting here, I reached out... and touched life....a circle of living, forever.

"Life's Little Patient Messages" **No. 3**

I sat in a different atmosphere, and aura, at a restaurant near where I used to work. One fine day in December 2001, in VA.,.... USA, I saw people there as professionals and glorified office workers, hurriedly pressing on to another level in the day, on their faces they wore a look of direction.

The strange thing was that even though... many of them knew me not they were for the most part polite, and into the winter holiday spirit. The concertos played on the speakers as window watchers glanced often from their meal to observe the passerby's intentions.

What an atmosphere though, to write, and get more in tune to the world around me. As I've said, it's where I used to work, so I drift off into Netherlands, not being in tune to the workplace. It could be the start of something big...just to sit, and watch people go by, with their cares as I whisper a silent prayer for.... them, as they venture in and out of the restaurant. Oh, the adrenaline flow, as the music... reaches a high point then drop, whilst I think on the Lord...and His goodness to me.

It's not in the universally played music, but in Jesus Christ of Whom I believe...and serve. The world will hear what and whomever it will hear, their prerogative is of their choice, just show love, and then move on. I hope this trip here today has touched even the solemn faced person, if by chance it didn't I at least expressed love, and a smile...that I possess.

"Life's Little Patient Messages" No. 4

This little message was given me by my parents and it goes as this, my dad used to say to me be dignified, show respect, and to hold up the family name. Also, he said business, and friendship doesn't mix, and if you play with a puppy, he'll lick you in your mouth. Blood is thicker than water, that's another famous saying, I was told personally, and that, what you don't start with you won't have to end with. My dad told me a lot of things, as action will speak louder than words, mind you these are the things my dad told to as a child and it is... there in my mind and heart, I'm thankful.

My mother told me a lot too, I think it is a part of "Life's Little Patient Messages" I think sometimes we hear them, and not take heed. My mother personally told me if you want something done right, then do it yourself. She said to always help people for you know not when you will need help, she also said, don't give somebody something you don't want yourself.

Things like, use what you've got, came to me from my mother, and my father, and give a man a honest day's work did too. I learned from my mother that I had to have a strong constitution, and from dad I was told that, the eagle flies high but he must come down to eat. What do this have to do with poetry and life? Well, what's in this book derived from...loving caring parents.

* *

" Let Freedom Ring! "

(Part I)

In this nation some saw a dream that we do need to keep alive,
Even though we have progressed, we have yet to arrive.

The dream of freedom and to hear it ring every where in hearts,
It would never happen if we or someone never starts.

Let's hold this dream very dear and at times just share,
And let others know that this privileged dream is there.

We need to keep also the hope alive and well unto this day,
As we listen to what all of the people in the world has to say.

An educational dream with equal rights in the plan,
To educate the women, men, boys, girls and every man.

Be it a great thing to have a freedom of rights signed and sealed,
We think so, and let the reminder allow this great nation to be healed.

* *

" Let Freedom Ring! "

(Part I I)

Talk of eloquence and firm speech with
a heart of desired love,
By the Hand of God, a free nation all the
way from the Lord above.

It's in the air and we feel the vibes of a
standardized right,
Given to us as we press forward to truly
continue the fight.

Now it's not a fight with hands, that's...
not in the nation's plan,
Remember now the nation talked about
peaceful freedom of every man.

We just want to ever dwell in the quiet
peace of our nation,
So that we will be so strong and able to
brave any situation.

It's of a lovely way to be at peace with
our dear hearts and minds,
So that our neighboring countries will
be happy with what it finds.

We should see this need, and the quality
of living in the whole thing,
Let the voice of love, peace and harmony
be heard.... and "Let Freedom Ring!"

* *

" Mother "

Blessed woman with love of gold, taking
care of her family with all her skills of old.
The love that she has keeps everything
together at best, she prays often and leave
to God the rest.

What gives her so much perseverance the
Lord only knows, as the love of "Mother"
to the world shows.
For God has now blessed her and guides
her along the way, and in the fullness of
the power of God, she diligently stay.

" Father "

What a blessed man and his stamina is
amazingly true, for years and years, he
has taken care of his family anew.
Everyday he presses his way to work,
out of responsibility and care, even if he's
retired, he has paid dues and been there.

He cuddles his family and protects them
by his concern, as years from now he will
see what his family will learn.
Being blessed of God, his love just stay
in stride, his family is blessed of him with
God as his guide.

* *

" Daughter "

An individual unique within herself,
Using all of her qualities, not leaving
them on the shelf.
She looks well to her parents and bless
them in every way,
Stopping by to say hello or just calling
them by phone every day.
Knowing and feeling the love that her
parents really need,
Has blessed her immensely, prompting
her to succeed.
A flow of love, and actions has always
been her lot, as she cares for her parents,
for they're the only ones she's got.
God has lead her since times past, being
lead of the Lord it certainly will last.

" Son "

Full speed ahead he looks forward to
blessing his parents today, he seek to
please them always in every way.
Chores around the house or a little
mechanical work at times, he chips in
and helps out it really has no rhymes.
Blessed of God he's lead along and is
precious in his parent's sight, this child
wants for his parents, what seems right.

* *

" Grandchildren "

When we look back into time, there's no rhythm or rhyme. For grandparents have always loved these little ones too, there's not anything that they for their "Grandchildren" wouldn't do.

Lots of love and caring showed as they put their "Grandchildren" under their wing, that's why they're so happy and they sing.
God has blessed the "Grandchildren" and they know that they're blessed of old, especially to have grandparents, with hearts of gold.

" Grandparents "

These blessed people are cherished by their children and grandchildren too, their family look to them as mentors from what they do.
They have sacrificed, that their family may be blessed, God has blessed these people to have truly passed the test.

They're loved, it shows over the children's and grandchildren's face, they've received of God what it took to run the race.
Being blessed continuously they go on their way, so learn from them, and what their life has to say.

* *

" Parents "

It had to start somewhere and that
a long time ago,
If it wasn't for the grandparents of
old we would not even know.

These blessed people of " Mother "
and " Father ", however their lot,
Always seemed to manage support,
and give us what they've got.

Through storms of life they stood by
us, and steadily stand by us today,
All in all we're grown, but childhood
memories always stay.

Blessed of God, these people with
hearts of sweet caring ways,
Will be loved of their children, and
that for many days.

God bless the new " Parents " and
" Parents " of old times past,
Rear your children in love, and the
fellowship will last.

These poems have been taken from the poetry book, "Inspirational Heartfelt Poems" Book V Poem Collection By Florence Camp Jackson

* *

" Sister "

A blessed child in the family and sent
by God above, sent to share, uplift, and
show her love.
She will help you along the way, by her
wisdom and skills, helping you over many
enormous hills.
So precious her embrace, her comforting
words, all because of what she's taught,
and heard.
So anyone that has a "Sister" is so truly
blessed, for she will be there beside you to
help you pass the test.

" Brother "

God knows the blessing that we need,
For brothers are sent to help us succeed.
He helps in more ways than one could
ever name,
It's the way he's been taught all the same.
He will be there for you with an embrace
and a gentle pat on the back,
Even, if he's tired physically, he will give
you no slack.
So we know the blessing of having a fine
"Brother," like this one,
And to see him in my presence, is as being
welcomed as the morning sun.

* *

" Granddaughter "

So grand is the word of all the granddaughters
in this world, a blessing from my family, even
a wonderful girl.
She has the array of love, and kindness to her
grandparents evermore, from days of old her
work spoke as I thought I told you so.

I knew that she would be a blessing to me, sent
from God above, her life is enhanced with great
humbleness of character, and her duties of love.

I thank the Lord for a "Granddaughter"... as
the one that was sent to me, and the blessing of
the whole thing is here for the world to see.

" Grandson "

Oh, the blessing that has been bestowed to me,
the kindness, love and support that come to be.
Of my family this child was truly sent one day,
I Wouldn't have wanted it to be any other way.

He says, kind words to his grandparents, and
he makes them feel grand, I thank God that he
grew up to be a fine young man.
Hope follows him as he's so concerned about
the others and us, by the life he lives, it shows
that in God he has trust.

* *

" Niece "

**Further along she will realize her worth,
She finds that she's blessed since birth.
She loves her family, and it really shows,
It's an array of goodness, the world knows.
Blessings are upon her head from the Lord
up above, and she will stay rooted as taught
in God's love.**

" Nephew "

**A precious mother's, and a father's son,
Tells the world of the battles he's won.
He is much appreciated, he made a name.
A good name of his parents, all the same.
He's a blessing as he goes about his way,
He's taught of his parents to, in God stay.**

" The Family Tree "

**All set in array, all in a row, all precious
loved ones that we know. From our great,
grandparents of days of old, to the days of
our parents as we were told.
There was a line of fine people, and strong
willed too, if not it would not have lasted as
long, like me and you.**

* *

" Aunt "

Oh, the teachings that was ministered to
me, you took the time out, so I'd be free.
Saying to me, watch out now for things
that you've heard, staying in the Master
up above and His Word. Balancing things
always everyday, for you're a blessing ...
sent to me in every way.

" Uncle "

Yes, you have taught me, and I've learned,
taught too, of the good and bad, to discern.
I'm safely in the blessings of God that you
did share, these things come to me because
you care. You're blessed in the Lord above,
you're rooted and grounded in His love.

" Cousin "

Oh, what an array of blessings that has
come to us, for years we've in God trust.
Beautiful people, girls, boys, women and
men, which have held our family together
to win. A lot of likeness along the line, as
a "Cousin," they're mine. We're together,
some more close than others, yet we treat
each other like sisters and brothers.

* *

" Making The Best Of Life "

Sometimes in life we feel so all alone,
It's as if sometimes, all hope is gone.
Yet, God gives us all our needs, and much grace,
Therefore, sometimes lonely, but not alone, to run this race.

We must learn to stand upon our very own two feet,
And to never in life through trials, ever admit defeat.

Fight on, go on, with your life at best,
For God will always, give you grace to pass life's tests.

So you're " Making The Best Of Life " and doing alright,
When you, with God's help, don't give up the fight.

" Rays Of Intelligence "

As the sun shines, hope is renewed. God up above sheds His love. Now a rebound of peace flourishes, as the peacemakers, with wisdom move on.

* *

" A Good Compassionate Few "

I call to remembrance the days of
yesteryears,
When we had the sense of direction,
and people's hearts were so dear.

We talk of good people, and their
array of hope and love,
Yet, it all came from God up above.

Someone to show mercy, and love to
all people alike,
Do your deeds in the blessing of alms,
and not spread it on the mike.

Through the times in this life, there's
still "A Good Compassionate Few,"
It all starts with God, and people like
...me and you.

All Poems on pages 181-197 have been taken from the Poetry Book, "Inspirational Heartfelt Poems, Book V" Poem Collection By Florence Camp Jackson
(Authors, Same)– Florence Rosie Givens

The poems in this book are for your reading enjoyment, and for entertainment purposes only. I only wrote the story of my own life in my own words and also about life itself with God's Grace...and Friends, Forever.

Thank you for your time and effort and for your patronage in reading, and purchasing this book. Hopefully, it has fared better in your spare time to read happy, smooth.... flowing, peaceful poems...of every day subjects and of nature.

After reading this book and you would... now like to pass it along to friends just the thought is nice...yet, remember...it's readable over and over again. In the seasons to come, especially in the winter, cozy type... seasons, it would make a good companion.

Where will your copy be?......be it better by your side, alongside other books sought out for your reading pleasure...I know for God's Word leads me in a way to search... forever for pleasant words of wisdom that build my character every day, toward His Mercy and Grace, unto eternal life....with Him, forevermore.

"The Ring Of Friends: Forever"...can be obtained, by doing the following: surfing the Website: www.floboundpoems.com by e-mail: MorningPoemsFloG@aol.com, by the Website: www.gospelandgifts.com by the Website: www.amazon.com .....also visit Gospel and Gifts Towne Books, that's located at: 2852 #103 Jefferson Davis Hwy., town of Stafford, VA., USA 22554. Toll free number is 1-800-720-1720 for the bookstore. Thank you again, for your patronage. F.R.G.

* *

Time For An Uplift...... Scripture Reading

Psalm 104:23 KJV
23 Man goeth forth unto his work
and to his labour until the evening.

Proverbs 17:17 KJV
17 A friend loveth at all times, and a
brother is born for adversity.

Proverbs 27:17 KJV
17 Iron sharpeneth iron; so a man
sharpeneth the countenance of his
friend.

Proverbs 27:19 KJV
19 As in water face answereth to
face, so the heart of man to man.

Proverbs 15:13 KJV
13 A merry heart maketh a cheerful
countenance: but by sorrow of the
heart the spirit is broken.

Proverbs 16:24 KJV
24 Pleasant words are as an honeycomb,
sweet to the soul, and health to the bones.

St. Luke 1:37 KJV
37 For with God nothing shall be impossible.

Stay encouraged...find some encouragement.

About The Author

"The Ring Of Friends: Forever" © 2002
Poem Collection By Florence Rosie Givens

Now that we realize that "The Ring Of Friends: Forever" will be there...... we rest in peaceful resolve and freedom...feeling free.... about life. Florence Rosie Givens, is a messenger of cheer, and encouragement to those who will hear. We can get on with our lives.....for life is short but blessed. Givens, enjoys her 4 children of which she is very ecstatic about, they're also friends. She has pressed over her trials of a former.... single parent, yet hope never left her side and neither....did God ever fail, and never will He fail. We reach some low ebb tides, in our lives but we must overcome.
When your life is set before you and you see no way out at present......keep holding on to your integrity. God is a present help to us all....only believe. Trust God...this is about Poetry.....but also about life, getting through our lives, in a victorious manner...is a desire for some.

Florence Rosie Givens is author, editor...and publisher of three books of Poem Collections. She has nine copyrighted books of Poetry, and have braved the storms of life to include...... a brief history of her life, and other words of wisdom in..."The Ring Of Friends: Forever." Givens, resides in Virginia, USA.,.... with her husband, Josephus. Just be you... be happy.